Successfully Start Your Business:

Expert Advice from a Business Broker

By Andrew Rogerson

Certified Business Intermediary (CBI)
Certified Business Broker (CBB)
Certified Machinery and Equipment Appraiser (CMEA)
Certified Senior Business Analyst (CSBA)

www.Andrew-Rogerson.com

Published by

RBS

Rogerson Business Services
Sacramento, CA
www.businesstransactionbooks.com

Rogerson Business Services
777 Campus Commons Road, Suite 200
Sacramento, CA, 95825
www.businesstransactionbooks.com

Successfully Start Your Business: Expert Advice from a Business Broker
Copyright © 2008-2009 Andrew Rogerson, CBI, CBB, CMEA, CSBA

ISBN: 978-1-4775460-1-7

Library of Congress Registration Number: TX-7-071-315

Disclaimer

This publication is designed to provide accurate and helpful information on starting a new business. It is sold with the understanding that the author is NOT engaged in offering legal, accounting, or any other professional advice. Please consult a competent professional for assistance.

Acknowledgements

Business Brokerage Press
Business Brokerage by Lloyd R Manning
International Franchise Association (IFA)
The Business Reference Guide by Tom West
International Business Brokers Association (IBBA)
California Association of Business Brokers (CABB)
International Franchise Association (IFA) Franchise University
Roger Murphy at Murphy Business and Financial Corporation, Clearwater, FL
The Resource Handbook for Business Brokers and Intermediaries by Tom West
Ultimate Guide to Personal Finance for Entrepreneurs by Peter Sander with J Jeff Lambert

Special Thanks

Special thanks to the following for contributing to the text and/or checking the details: Anne Rogerson, Roger Murphy, Tim Rogers, Greg Roquet, Stephanie Chandler, Jerry Tsai, Tom Miller, Diane Miller, Fred Hall, Nick Kalfountzos "The Graphics Man," and Belinda Rogerson for her editing suggestions.

Extra Special Thanks

Also, an extra special thanks to Anne Rogerson and Belinda Rogerson for their editing and work on the website.

Special Acknowledgment of IBBA

The International Business Brokers Association is a global organization that advances the professional development of over 1,800 member intermediaries, educates potential clients about the value of intermediary services, and promotes the highest possible standards of ethical conduct. IBBA sponsors national education programs and conferences twice each year and cooperates with state and local business broker's organizations to conduct "grass roots" programs for the benefit of business communities around the country. IBBA awards the prestigious designation of Certified Business Intermediary (CBI) to members who demonstrate professional excellence through their intermediary experience and education and pass a comprehensive examination. Andrew Rogerson holds the CBI designation.

For more information contact:

International Business Brokers Association
401 North Michigan Avenue, 24th Floor
Chicago, IL 60611-4267
Phone: 888-686-4222   Fax: 312-673-6599
E-mail: admin@ibba.org
Web: www.ibba.org

Special Acknowledgment of CABB

The California Association of Business Brokers is a professional trade association whose members are actively involved in assisting their clients in buying, selling, and evaluating businesses. CABB was organized to recognize the professionals of business opportunity brokerage, to help educate the public on the benefits of using licensed intermediaries, and to establish a code of ethics to which members adhere. CABB awards the prestigious designation of Certified Business Broker (CBB) to members who demonstrate professional excellence through their intermediary and business brokerage experience and education and pass a series of examinations. Andrew Rogerson holds the CBB designation.

For more information contact:

California Association of Business Brokers
1215 K Street, Suite 2290
Sacramento, CA, 95814
Phone: 866-972-2220 Fax: 916-231-2141
E-mail: cabb@cabb.org
Web: www.cabb.org

Table of Contents

Welcome!

When an entrepreneur first decides to look at business ownership, it generally sets off a series of complex and confusing questions as well as an emotional roller coaster. The complex and confusing questions include…Will I buy an existing business? If it's existing it's already an existing business it should be established and therefore come with less risk. What about buying a franchise, that may be easier as I then have the franchisor to help me? How about I start my own business, I can then do it my way? If I start my own business, what will I do and will it be successful? The bottom line is that it's already pretty confusing and hard to decide.

Because business ownership has three different paths we can take, this workbook is built for one purpose only and that is to help a business owner who is considering starting their own business. Lots of would-be entrepreneurs go down this path. Many stop before they really get going for many reasons, while many start but don't conclude the journey as they run out of time, money, enthusiasm or all of these reasons combined, or for other reasons. A separate workbook is available on buying an existing business and is called Successfully Buy Your Business: Expert Advice from a Business Broker. If your decision is made to buy a franchise then please look for my workbook called Successfully Buy Your Franchise: Expert Advice from a Business Broker.

If this workbook has one purpose it has two goals. The first goal is to outline and inform about the different tasks and questions a business owner starting from scratch will have to make as they move through the decision making process. The second and most important goal is to encourage the business owner starting their business from scratch to make all decisions that at any time during the ownership, management and operation of their business, the business they are building should be ready for immediate sale to a motivated buyer. Perhaps I can hear you gasp – that doesn't make much sense, but obviously I beg to differ. And let me explain why. I think most would agree that we go into business to make money. The money allows us to live our lifestyle and follow our dreams. No argument from me there. It's my suggestion, based on my experience as a 5 time business owner and as a business broker, that you will get more money for your business if you discipline yourself to operate the business and have it always "buyer ready" than try to sell the business when it suits you. I see too many business owners trying to exit business ownership when the economy is declining or they have health, family, personal, employee problems etc, and so the final price they get from the business is much less.

The inspiration for this guide comes from my personal experiences in buying, selling, owning and operating five businesses in two countries, researching many, many different types of businesses, and my current experience as a business consultant/broker to those that wish to exit or enter business ownership. I wish someone had given me some organized structure to tackle this difficult experience as I have had to learn it the hard way. Now my goal is to help make that journey easier for you.

Please use this workbook to make notes along the way. This is a guide to read, learn, and stimulate. Scribble ideas and inspirations you have and check them out later so you don't lose your thoughts and are therefore ultimately better prepared. If you prefer to make lots of notes before finalizing your thoughts, photocopy the pages so you can have one final version to work through as you arrive at different decision points.

Starting a business from scratch requires unique skill, patience, courage, money, and good old fashioned hard work. So be patient as you travel your journey...though without question, the rewards are wonderful. And I wish you nothing but success.

Your Goals

Use the chart below to write down major tasks that come to mind that you feel you must do to successfully start your business. Refer back to this chart as you read through this guide so that you can add tasks you want to complete and stay up-to-date.

Task Description	Start Date	Completion Date

Idea Tracker

As you read this guide, it will inspire ideas or prompt action items. Use the space below to jot down and track these ideas so you can organize your thoughts into action items.

Your Feedback

The goal of this guide is to help business owners through the process of starting their business in the quickest time possible and maximize the return they make when they sell their business or perhaps more accurately, work on their business continuously so it's always ready for sale. Although all business owners have the same objective—to operate their business for maximum return on investment and then either sell it or pass it on to the next generation - the journey to achieving that goal is never the same.

There are a wide variety of factors that affect the entire process:

- ✓ Each have unique personal differences be it the type of industry they chose, whether they want a service or product-driven business or the amount of money available to buy a business etc.
- ✓ The business background the buyer comes from.
- ✓ The professional support services the buyer chooses to consult or hire.
- ✓ The current direction of the economy.
- ✓ The current state of the industry the buyer chooses to enter.
- ✓ If finance is required and the source of that finance, be it family and friends or institutions such as banks or credit unions.
- ✓ Taxes and related laws that often change.

Because of these factors and many others, I strongly advise you to seek the assistance of experts at different stages of your business ownership journey. We'll cover these as we work through the different phases but help from a person with financial experience is always a great idea as well as help from an attorney experienced with business laws.

If you have comments or suggestions that you feel would improve this guide and you have a moment to share, please e-mail your suggestions to info@Andrew-Rogerson.com.

With thanks,

Andrew Rogerson

The Golden Rule

While you run your business and make each of your decisions, do so in the context that your business is always for sale.

General Information

> *"The future belongs to people that see possibilities before they become obvious."*
>
> *Ted Levitt*

Introduction

The steps to starting a new business are numerous, almost always complex and at times, very frustrating. Most of the decisions are logical and straightforward and sequential, that is, you can only go from A to C via B. As I said in the Welcome, the major purpose of this guide is to tease out the many steps in starting a new business and put them in some sort of logical order. But most critically and what I see rarely done, is to also have the owner of the business make those steps in the context of disciplined decisions that include the benefit of whether or not that decision is adding value to the business and thereby adding value should a buyer wish to purchase the business today. With this background, this guide can reduce the number of steps or missteps that you may take, thereby reducing the costs, time spent, complexity and frustration. Starting, owning, and operating a business is not for everyone. But hopefully following these steps, it will allow you to make that determination on your own, as there are great personal, financial and emotional rewards in business ownership, most of which are only realized once the business is sold.

Additionally, this guide is written from a different perspective. It is not written from the perspective of an accountant, attorney, financial planner, business coach, landlord or employee, but that of a business broker. My current profession is that of a business broker. I help business owners exit business ownership or buyers enter business ownership. I get into the nitty gritty of a business and see what's happening, what's done well, what could be done better, and how both sides in the transaction always seeing things differently but with my job to bring everyone together. It is this perspective I bring to this guide. The questions I ask, the processes I suggest and the dynamic I bring, also comes from my business brokering experience.

And remember this guide is built for work. Make notes and use the templates to jot down ideas as they come to mind so you can refer back to them. The starting of your business is unique. One of the main reasons for publishing this in workbook format is so that you can write in it, customize, and use the information to be successful in starting your business in the quickest time possible.

The flow of the guide is as follows:
- ✓ Section One provides some general information on some of the concepts and terms you may come across when thinking about starting a new business.
- ✓ Section Two educates on different skills and personnel you may need.
- ✓ Section Three covers planning so you can build strong foundations to see if truly starting your business is your best option, as well as incorporate some of the topics covered earlier.
- ✓ Sections Four deals with the task of starting your business from theoretical to practical, while Section Five looks at additional resources and tools that may be of interest to you.

Please write down any terms you come across that aren't familiar to you. If they aren't covered in the glossary, you are welcome to e-mail them to me at info@Andrew-Rogerson.com and I will add them to the next edition of the guide. You are also welcome to e-mail questions about starting your business.

Tip: Write down your inspirations

Starting a business is a creative process. Never lose an idea because it was forgotten. Write down your ideas so you can ultimately accept or reject them.

Business Ownership – What Are My Options?

So you've decided to consider starting your own business. Before we get too deep into that, let's have a look at your options. Basically there are only three options. First, start a business from scratch with your own idea, second, buy an existing business or third, try a combination of one and two and buy the rights to a franchise to open it from scratch.

Below is a table that captures each of the three options and then attempts to lay out the different risks or variables associated with each idea. I've included this table to give you some talking or thinking points to see if you can find one option that makes more sense to you than the other. The list below is not exhaustive so please use the table on the next page to add other ideas that are important to you. It may create action items for you to research further so write them down as well. If you have questions, challenges, suggestions or simply want to vent, please email me at info@andrew-rogerson.com

	Start new business	*Buy existing business*	*Buy a franchise*
Availability	None	Limited	Many
Established business methodologies	None	Hopefully	Yes
Documented processes	None	Limited - if at all	Yes
Training	None	Initial 2 weeks or so	Initial and ongoing
Investment V Profit	None	Yes	None
Support during ownership	None	None	Yes
Risk	Highest	Unknown until you're the owner	Many variables
Finance availability	Very difficult	Yes	Yes
How to predict success	Success based on projections	Success comes from history only	Success based on feedback from current owners
Decision maker	Owner	Owner	Follow the system
Instant cash flow	No	Yes	No
Established customer relationships	No	Yes	No
Established relationship with suppliers	No	Yes	Maybe
Established reputation	No	Yes	Yes
Established brand	No	Yes	Yes

Use the table below to write down additional ideas you consider important to include when deciding which business option to pursue

Idea	Start new business	Buy existing business	Buy a franchise

Write down any ideas you want to research further.

How Do I Know If Starting A Business Is Right For Me?

This is possibly a burning question as you consider different options, especially if what you are currently doing is not rewarding and want to do something else. What are your options? Do you find a new job, stay in your current position or do you move into business ownership? As you look for answers to this question I suggest there may be many suggestions from those around you but ultimately the final answer will come from you and you alone. Deciding if starting a business from scratch and therefore business ownership is right for you includes many emotions and motivations. These may include:

- ✓ No more layoffs
- ✓ Having control of your work and personal life
- ✓ Having balance with work, family and friends
- ✓ Financial security
- ✓ Personal fulfillment
- ✓ Success
- ✓ Creating and building something
- ✓ Contributing to the community
- ✓ Family involvement
- ✓ No company politics
- ✓ Less frustration and job stress
- ✓ Getting away from corporate life

And perhaps I forgot the most important one – money. I think a major reason most people enter business ownership is because they believe they can make more money than what they currently doing and perhaps in the foreseeable future. What's interesting is that according to the book, the Millionaire Next Door, five out of six millionaires do so through business ownership.

How else do I decide?

Part of the purpose of this guide is to take you through the process so you can decide if starting a business from scratch makes sense to you - to allow you to arrive at the decision that makes sense to you. Not your spouse. Not your parents, family, best friend, neighbor, accountant, mentor, coach, consultant or advisor…but YOU.

But here are some other things to consider:

Goals

I think you would agree that all successful people have goals. I suspect that even unsuccessful people have goals, they perhaps lack the discipline, risk management skills, organizational skills, personal drive, education, chutzpah or perhaps they are unlucky. Or maybe they are on the path to success but just haven't got there yet. Whatever, if you've decided business ownership is something you want to consider, I expect the underlying drive is that you have goals and you see business ownership as the means to get there, but one of the underlying goals you have is personal wealth.

Entrepreneur V Intrapreneur

On page 14 we mentioned the 3 ways of entering business ownership – start from scratch, buy an existing business or start a franchise. (Yes, can you can buy an existing franchise but that's covered by option two.)

Perhaps the way to work out the best option for you is by a process of elimination. The key ingredients, I would suggest to successfully **start a new business** include:

1. A business idea not currently in the market or an improvement on an existing idea. Your goal is to have the market pay you enough money not only for the time you spend getting the project operational but also a return on your investment with any capital you need to invest.
2. The money to fund your business idea plus keep you fed, clothed and housed until you turn it into a commercial success.
3. The complete business skills package to develop the idea and perfect it and then build and deploy the sales and marketing, operation, management and financial systems to turn a profit.
4. The personality, education, personal skills and drive to see this through to a profit.

If you are unsure if this is the right option for you, there are two other workbooks available in this same series. The first is called "Successfully buy your franchise: Expert advice from a Business Broker" or the second, "Successfully buy your business: Expert advice from a Business Broker."

To help make the right decision about whether to buy an existing business, buy a franchise or start from scratch, consider the following:
Are you an Entrepreneur or an Intrapreneur?

My perception is that most main street or small business owners are either an entrepreneur or an intrapreneur. I see Entrepreneurs that own and run their own business and with the following characteristics:

- ✓ Highly independent
- ✓ Visionary
- ✓ Comfortable accepting higher risks
- ✓ Somewhat of a loner

I see Intrapreneurs that own and run their own business with the following characteristics:

- ✓ Tend to be more conservative
- ✓ Open to expert guidance
- ✓ Often more methodical, tending to mitigate risks
- ✓ Worked in Corporate America; possibly in a management role and so understands reporting structures, accountability, project timelines and working to achieve deadlines
- ✓ Tend to gravitate to the franchise business model as it provides structure and systems already built and in place.

But how do I really know if business ownership is right for me?

From the research I've done and from my personal experience, I honestly don't think there is a black and white answer. I think the hardest part of deciding to pursue business ownership is actually making that decision, as you don't know the answer until you start.

My decision to move into business ownership came from the lack of alternatives. I looked at the bosses I'd worked for and the people I knew in small business, and concluded that I could do all and sometimes more than the bosses I reported to. I then looked at people I knew in business ownership and decided I could match what they did if I paid attention to detail, sought opinions from those that were successful, and believed in myself.

A few other thoughts.

A critical ingredient of successful business owners that I have been able to observe is a personality trait of being a positive thinker. Running and owning a business is not easy, especially if there are self doubts. Having a positive attitude that looks through those difficult times is a very important attribute.

Another critical thing I did was understand that business ownership came with risks. My success would be increased if I managed the risk of running a business by paying everyone when they were due, making sure the customer's expectations were exceeded, did my best to have happy and motivated employees, and paying attention to detail.

Perhaps the final critical ingredient is having the support of those immediately around you such as your spouse and immediate family. Because they know who you are and understand you the best, they can support you when there are challenges running a business, and I am yet to talk to a business owner who hasn't experienced challenges. As they say, if it was easy everyone would do it.

So how do you really know if business ownership is right for you? You don't. In the Aboriginal community of Australia they have a saying, No Dream, No Story, No Song. Dreaming is a critical part of Aboriginal life in Australia. The significance of dreaming is that it's used to inspire positive emotions to take action. The Aboriginal communities love telling stories. Because of their isolated environment and the fact they are nomadic meant that books were not part of their culture. However their culture is critical to them both individually and collectively. And the way to educate their children and pass on their culture is through stories. The stories were about drought, flood, hunting, food and survival in one of the most inhospitable places in the world. Finally, the other way of passing things on and remembering things is through song. Like a book, a song would be used to explain an historic event or even to give directions. Water is critical in the remote parts of Australia. If you don't have a book or a map, how do you give directions to food or water? You do it through a song that explains how to get from point A to point B and how long it all takes.

So the point of the above is that either you believe in yourself and believe in your dream of business ownership and go for it, or no dream, no story, and no song.

Consider a SCORE counselor

Perhaps you would welcome talking to a SCORE counselor. SCORE is a non-profit organization that provides counseling services for potential or existing small business owners. They have local chapters throughout the United States where you can make an appointment with a counselor and get their advice for free on business ownership including operating, marketing, financial advice etc. They have a website at http://www.score.org where you can go to get more information and also easily navigate to their local chapter and phone or email to make an appointment to visit one of their counselors or advisors.

6 Personality Traits Of An Entrepreneur

This is an interesting topic in its own right but way beyond the scope of this workbook to address in too much depth. However, from the research I've done there seems to be agreement that the right personality traits may lead to a higher rate of success for would-be entrepreneurs. Here are some personality traits that may be good to have if you want to be an entrepreneur.

1. *Natural intelligence*
   Being a genius is not essential. Similarly, too much education can be a hindrance. Limited or impacted intelligence will invariably provide failure.
2. *Strong leadership*
   This helps as the business develops not only by attracting people who want to work for the entrepreneur, but also assuring customers, suppliers and other business leaders related to the business.
3. *Hard work ethic*
   Almost without exception, successful businesses come from hard work.
4. *Independent thinkers*
   This is an interesting trait as it captures different things. For example, the ability to come up with an idea is part of it, but also the courage and ability to focus on where the business is going as opposed to being told by "experts" that its going in the wrong direction.
5. *Street wise*
   This trait captures a few skills. These include the ability to think on their feet; understand hidden agenda, and when and when not to trust others.
6. *Motivation to succeed*
   This is probably one of the key ingredients for success. If you lack any of the above, but this ingredient is high then the chances of success are higher.

Some good news

The good news is that the following do not influence whether or not you will be successful as an entrepreneur. These traits are:

1. Age
2. Sex
3. Marriage
4. Education

Colonel Sanders was not deterred by his age of 62 in building one of the largest fried chicken businesses. Sex or gender is no longer an excuse; perhaps it could be argued that being a woman is in fact a plus. And as for education, we all know Bill Gates dropped out from Harvard during his sophomore year and Sir Winston Churchill never had an education higher than grade 3.

Final thought

If knowing whether or not you have the personal traits to be a successful entrepreneur are important to you, search the web for "Entrepreneur traits" or "Entrepreneur personality" etc. There are many articles on the topic but remember, whether or not you have the personal traits may be or may not be important, but what is critical is being able to take action. No action = no result.

What Sort Of Business Should I Start And When?

Deciding to start and own a business doesn't normally happen on a certain day of the week, at a certain time, nor indeed at a certain age. If the idea makes sense it's something that generally grows on to the point where you have to decide if that is the direction you wish to go. Few people are fortunate enough to be certain of their destinies early in life while the rest of us are forced to do some soul searching when the idea comes along. Regardless, there is great personal, professional and of starting a business hits.

In Section 7 we are going to cover the 7 stages of a business life cycle. If your idea of starting a business morphs into a reality, your new business will enter the economy when it is in one of its cycles. At the time of writing this guide, the US economy is in a recession and has been so officially for 12 months. So it would make sense that now is not the best time to start a new business? You should wait for the economy to start to recover? These are important questions to consider but not dwell on too long. If you wait for the economy to recover then you may start the business too late or too soon for the next part of the cycle or the industry you've chosen to enter may not be affected by the economic cycle but in fact time it perfectly. The bottom line is that it's important that you recognize where the economy is but not critical. It's more important that you determine your financial resources to make sure you have the capacity to keep going so you can adjust your business as it goes through the economic cycles. That's what it's all about; managing your risk. If you can manage your business through the economic cycles you will be successful.

If you're thinking about a business of your own but you're not sure where to start, here are several ideas that may ignite a creative spark for you.

1. *What are your interests, talents, and skills?*

What gets you out of bed each morning? Hopefully they are positive things but if they are not, that's OK too, as the goal of this task is to find out what's important to you, decide what you want to move away from, and put in place a program of change. So use the template at the end of this topic and write down what you like and don't like about your current job, and jobs you've had in the past. Do you love helping people, knowing more than your work colleagues, analyzing business plans, pouring over financial records to find a mistake, getting your computer to network with as many computers on the other side of the world? Be creative and write your likes and dislikes so you can see with more clarity where some of your interests lie, and which tasks you want to avoid.

The goal is to be creative by brainstorming and mind mapping to arrive at business ideas and find one that you will be excited and motivated about to do on a regular basis and critically, one that will create a standard of living and lifestyle important to you and your family. If you don't like being chained to a desk, don't choose a business that requires you to be stuck in an office all day.

The exciting news is that you get to make these decisions for yourself. Perhaps you are good with finance and accounting and you're thinking about becoming a tax agent, but you prefer a business with a core component of sales. If you are serving clients in your area and because this will be your business, won't you also be required to meet with them? Could you find a way to meet with them at their place of business or over lunch?

Use the list you are creating to help identify your strengths and weaknesses. If you don't enjoy meeting with people, then probably a sales job is not the best place for you. Most businesses require a sales component and so that's the point of this exercise. Identify the core product or service that gets you out of bed, or you have a special talent and put it into a business plan (which we talk about in Section Three.) Focus on your strengths and weaknesses while recognizing that for the business to survive and thrive, as it grows you will need to hire different skills, and so a cost should be allocated to your budget for a sales person once you reach a certain level of profitability or cash flow.

Spend some time with this exercise and look for a theme in your lists. If you identify a business that interests you, but it doesn't meet your lifestyle requirements, then expand on the idea and see if there is a different type of business in that field that would suit you better. The ultimate goal is to find that core idea that works for you, put it into a business plan with a budget as well as a sales and marketing plan, and then productivity plan. But we'll get to that in more detail in Section Three.

2. Use the power of imagination

What would you do if you won the lottery for $100,000? Retiring is not an option as $100,000 isn't enough money to retire on, plus hopefully you have too many things in life you want to do. Use the power of imagination to let you think of creative ways to use that money to start a business. Write down ideas about how you could use it to build a website or lease a store or warehouse you've had your eye on but didn't take any action because it didn't make sense to take a risk. Imagine your life in retirement and you want to look back at what you did. Did you do all the things you wanted to do? Let's come back to the present. What does your ideal work life look like? What kind of business would you start if you had endless resources?

3. Do you have a gift, talent or hobby that could get you started in business?

As a child, perhaps you loved dancing, playing the guitar, collecting stamps, playing soccer, loved math in school or ran home from school to help Mom or Gran in the kitchen. Regardless, perhaps you could take this enthusiasm and use it to start a business. Perhaps your current job is a sales manager so why not combine your enthusiasm with your current skill, for example, start a business that promotes dancers or guitar players or stamps. Initially be creative, but keep it real. Also, if you found it interesting is it something that's fairly commonly known so there is a market for it. I lived and grew up in Australia and played a lot of cricket. Not sure I could make a business out of promoting cricket in the United States but perhaps I could make a business importing and selling Australian art or furniture or memorabilia. Think outside the box. Play around on the internet and Google for ideas. For example, if you have a gift for dance, search for "dance clothes" or "dance venues" and see if the results spark an idea. Perhaps you enjoy writing and want to write about dance, sell dance clothes for adults and children, specialize in photography for dancers or sell dance memorabilia.

4. Talk to your family and friends

This one can be a double edged sword, but ask the people closest to you for their thoughts on starting the ideal business. Be careful they don't unload what they would like to or conversely, look at you with a blank stare and say – why would you want to throw away what you've done and go into business? But you may gain a golden nugget or two and all you are looking for is one.

5. Try a new paradigm

A paradigm means seeing the world in a certain way based on experience or what you've been told. For example, if I use the word family it should evoke a series of words you would use to describe what a family looks like. Because we all have different experiences we will have different definitions of family. If you went to school and then college with the expectation of finishing and getting a job, and that's what you've done, you've lived your paradigm. If you've decided that there's more to life than working for somebody else, you are entering a paradigm shift where you want to break out of a preconceived set of ideas either you've placed on yourself, or others have placed on you. Your family paradigm may be that everyone works for a company. Trying to break out of that paradigm or mold can be tough but that's all it is – tough. Every business you see had to start somewhere by someone. The sandwich shop you visit weekly, the restaurant, the local mechanic shop all were born from somebody's dream. Pay attention to every business you encounter. Is the owner present? If so, does he or she look content? Worn out? Harried? Start talking to business owners you encounter. Ask them about the pros and cons of what they do. Most will be glad to talk if you catch them in a quiet moment and you'll realize they have no super skill other than a penchant for giving something a go and staying at it.

6. *Look for ideas in a bookshop and library*

Another great source of ideas is the local book store and library. Not only does it give you the best opportunity to learn, it shows you a vast world of knowledge that has been converted from an idea into a book. A book is a great example of a mini business. For the book to get to the book store or library, somebody had to have the idea and write about it. The idea was then submitted to a book publisher for them to decide if there was enough money in it to publish the book. Once it's published, it has to be distributed and promoted. All this costs money so those business people in the process are deciding if they can get a return on their investment and make a profit. So the ideas are in abundance at the local book store and library, simply look for them. As an additional idea, spend some time in the business section and read some of the books. You never know where you will find inspiration. Many business books list examples from real entrepreneurs. Perhaps one of these examples will spark your interest or cause you to think about something you hadn't considered before.

7. *Read Inc magazine, Success magazine and other business magazines.*

There are a lot of business magazines. Inc magazine and Success magazine are probably two of the best, but once again, visit your local bookstore or magazine stand to see the range of magazines available and see if you can find an inspiration. And don't just look for the business magazines. The range of magazines shows you the diversity of interests out there from health to photography to trucks to cooking and goes on. Use your imagination and you will find a magazine about it; or if you can't, perhaps there's a good business you can start..

8. *Haven't found the right idea?*

Giving up is the easy part. If you can't find the right idea don't be afraid to take a break and then come back to finding what makes sense to you. By doing this the idea may jump out at you. But don't give up! Running a business requires perseverance and so does looking for a business. In Section Three we are going to talk about having a life plan. Carve some time out every day to focus on your life plan. Get up 15 minutes earlier in the morning, take time out of your lunch hour or stay up an hour later, but whatever you do, devote some time to dreaming and writing down your future. If you are serious about moving forward, you will make the time.

Finally, be patient with yourself and the inspirations will come. Spend time reading business message boards, websites and magazines. On the next page is a template that you can use to jot down things that you like or don't like, strengths and weaknesses to see if this throws up opportunities. Be open to savoring ideas and then further research them to see if there is a fit. And here's a suggestion. What are your gifts? You love numbers or writing stories or collecting stamps or helping children or talking with the elderly or music or dance or photography or collecting junk or making meat pies or weeding the garden. Guess what – there is a business opportunity in all of those. Can you see it?

If you have a gift you have the start of a business. Simply look for it. It will reveal itself.

Task/responsibility	Like	Don't like	Strength	Weakness

10 "Musts" Before Starting Your Business

You have decided to start a business and chosen to be a mechanic. Your first thought is to market yourself and so you make some business cards, print a flyer and put an ad in the Yellow Pages (because that's what everyone else does.) You also get a website and a domain name that tells everyone why you are the best mechanic including your education, credentials, training and experience. You also put a sign in your local grocery store. And then you wait. And wait. And wait…

But unfortunately nothing happens. But, that's what everyone does, isn't it? Print out some brochures, tell everyone how great you are, and wait for the work to roll in and therefore the money.

Let's take a breath! What can we do to improve on this and therefore become successful a lot quicker and with a little less pain?

Must # 1:

First, being a "mechanic" is too general. There are a million mechanics in the world, but the only successful ones have something to concentrate on. A particular auto manufacturer, or particular age of auto, or particular region of auto, for example, European, Asian or American autos only. Be specialized - it pays more, shows an expertise and reduces the amount of training and re-training you need to do to stay on top of your specialty. You've heard the saying - "Jack of all trades, master of none."

Must # 2:

This is my favorite. If you fail to plan, you plan to fail. An idea is not a business plan, or a marketing plan, or even just a goal. It is simply an idea. Although the planning process may seem long and tedious now, it will benefit you more than you could imagine in the future. For example, when you need to talk to the bank to borrow some money, when you are planning to hire employees, when the phone finally rings and people ask "Do you do …" or "Can you …" you need to know if accepting this piece of business is right for you or something you are better not tackling just yet because you don't have the resources, capital, training or expertise etc. Your business plan is a road map to guide you, but not constrain you. If something in your plan doesn't fit just right, change it. Your business plan is a work in progress and constantly changes. This is the excuse most people use by not making a business plan, as they argue their plan always changes.

Must # 3:

Recognize that when you start your business one of your scarcest resources will be money. Therefore, the scarce amount of money you have must be spent wisely. Things that can quickly eat up your start-up funds which appear exciting to invest in, must be reviewed to make sure it's money well spent. For example, a cash drain can be brochures and extensive marketing materials. You need a good business card but as you are starting out, good will do. Make sure it has quality paper and presents well. A flashy logo or raised letters or other creative ideas that increase the price can come later when you get better feedback from the market. As the business evolves and gains traction you can invest more money in these items, but right now as you are starting out, you will spend far more producing them than they will produce for you. You can't afford to ignore the high cost of printing these materials, and the costs associated in designing them especially if you aren't proficient yourself. If your business is all about business cards and marketing material and this is your core competency and you are using your labor to design and innovate to showcase your product and service then go for it. However, most start-up businesses change too quickly for these materials to be effective for more than a short period, sometimes as little as days. If it costs $1000 to print these the first time, and $1000 to design them the first time, imagine how much you will pay if your brochures beat statistics and last 2 months. If alterations to design cost $500, it costs $1500 every time your business changes. If your business services change every 2 months while you are ironing out the kinks, you can expect to spend at least $9000 that year on brochures and business cards. Don't waste your time, or your money, on brochures and business cards until you can keep your typical sales presentation the same for at least 6 months. Otherwise, these things aren't worth the trouble.

Must # 4:

Advertising: If you start a new business you need to advertise. The first place you probably think to go is the Yellow Pages. Not so fast. If you start looking for your local Yellow Pages directories you may find ten, fifteen or more books. Now you look at the section that applies to the service that's of interest to you and you see how many other trillions of dog walkers there are. Which ad stands out? Definitely not the little ad in the corner and you missed the one-liner. When you are starting out you have to stretch your advertising dollars as far as you can. Consider waiting to year three before advertising in the Yellow Pages. By then you will have more sales and profit and probably a permanent address and website etc so you can take out the largest ad in that Yellow Pages so you stand out.

Must # 5:

Website: Everyone says you have to have a website. So you check the costs, proudly register your domain name, shell out money and time creating the site and wait for the customers. That's what the sales person from the web company said! When you start your business a website is a nice idea but it has to come when you have something to say, or more importantly, not only worked out what you want to say, but know it's what your customers are telling you they want to hear. Your business will take time to get established so you need to time to understand what to communicate to your customers. If you must have a website, try to design your own. If that doesn't work, get a friend or relative who knows what to do, create one for you at the lowest price possible. Once the business builds you can then gain traction on investing in a professionally built site. If neither of these options are working for you, have a professional create the difficult parts and hand it off to someone you know to do the routine parts. Websites are a great idea but they can be a time, money and energy drain especially if it requires constant changes and updates because your business is changing as you get more and better feedback from the market.

Must # 6:

Use your gift! Your education, friends, family or neighbors won't bother a customer. Your ability to provide something they can't or want to do themselves is what it's all about. If you have a gift, try to make that the basis of a business as by definition it means you can do it better than others. If you need inspiration, use the template on page 23 and take any of the words you've written down and simply Google them. See what pops up and it will give you a whole bunch of ideas that others may be doing – but you can do better.

Must # 7:

A good marketing consultant will get you to focus your skill on being in front of the people who want your service. McDonald's made a great success of marketing to the children and not the adults. They discovered that Mom and Dad wanted to be seen to be good to their kids so they would ask the kids – where do you want to eat? After the kids had seen all the advertising on TV for Ronald McDonald and what he ate, the answer was simple. Bottom line – market your service to the people that want and need it – not everybody as that is too expensive.

Must # 8:

This is probably the toughest part for a business starting out. You have limited cash to grow your business, so if things get tight the first cost to cut is marketing…and this can your biggest mistake. Whatever you do, try and continue some sort of marketing of your business. Even if it's low cost strategies like networking, public speaking, a low cost website, and an ad in a publication that corresponds to your target market. If you stop when you run out of new ideas, you probably won't get much. The key to marketing is repetition. Make sure people think of your name when they have a problem. If they have only seen your name once, but your competitor just sent them a third flier, your competitor will get their business. We've all heard that it takes more than once for a customer to buy. With the information available to your customers today, you want your name to be in front of them as much as possible.

Must # 9:

We've all heard the maxim – If you fail to plan you plan to fail. A similar maxim to this is that if you do nothing then you will have achieved your objective. Starting a business is particularly tough as there is so much to do and so little time. Find a way to motivate yourself and stay motivated! One of the best ways to do that is by using a Productivity Plan. This is talked about more in Section Three but a Productivity Plan is simple a "To do" list of things you want done. This can be a great motivator as you can look back after two weeks and review what you did and see how much you've done since. You will make mistakes; how else do we learn. But the challenge is to keep going so the mistakes become less, and as the tide of success flows with your business you ride that tide.

Must # 10:

Patience is a virtue - another great maxim we've all heard, but critically important for those starting a new business. Starting a new business will require creativity, stamina, and learning from your mistakes. Not every idea you have will work and work magnificently. Often it may be tweaking an idea but you won't know what that is until you try. Be confident, be determined, be energetic, but above all be patient.

Starting a business is one of the hardest things anyone can ever do. It comes with uncertainty, lack of a support structure, no road map, and probably against our natural tendencies to look for reassuring guideposts. However, the professional and personal rewards greatly outweigh the sacrifices, plus the things we learn allow us to be stronger and financially secure for the next steps of our journey.

Follow Your Dream - No Dream, No Story, No Song.

Starting a business from scratch is not for everyone. No question about it. One of my main goals in writing this guide is to provide as much information as possible in as logical order as possible so you, and only you, can make that final decision about whether you will start your own business. I'm sure you have read or heard before that someone once observed: "Everyone is an expert in at least two areas: telling you how to raise *your* kids and telling you how to lead *your* life." My children tell me that all the time. Perhaps there should be a third area: "others telling you how to run *your* business." Everyone loves to think they are helping - it's only human nature. Everyone has an opinion and we like nothing better than sharing their opinion – be it valuable or not. And because they deliver their opinion with such good intention, when we don't follow the advice we feel bad. Perhaps the hardest advice we get are the "horror" stories from people who are close to us. If you are thinking about starting your own business it will be a difficult decision and you will get naysayers. However, the bottom line is that it's your life; you get to make the final decision – and that's the way it should be.

So here are eight reasons you can use **not** to start your own business. Incidentally, I have explained why the eight reasons are not valid but once again, in the end you get to make that final decision – that's what following your dream is all about.

1. A 'loved one' or spouse dream killer:

This is probably the most important of them all. The business buyer talks it over with his loved one or significant other and thinks they have agreement they will start a new business. When the decision day comes the agreement is not as forthcoming as first thought as objections and concerns begin to flow.

Answer: Starting and owning a business must be a *joint decision*. Business ownership will impact your family in a way that having a job change doesn't. If it's scary for you, imagine how it must feel to those around you. They have less information about what you are thinking of doing or they may not be as informed. Even before the search begins, a married couple needs frank, honest discussions about the benefits and problems of business ownership.

2. The "Passion" dream killer:

Often you will hear or read that you must have a "passion" for your product or service. And if you don't have that passion, don't get involved. How much passion can you maintain doing the same thing day in and day out?

Answer: There are two important points. First, you are running a business and it's your responsibility as the owner to run it correctly by following the appropriate laws, ensuring customer service is as high as possible, all the bills are paid etc. If you don't run the business properly then everything goes away. Second, the "passion" you need is building a viable and ongoing business so you can feed and maintain you and/or your family and then make some money when you sell your business. *Passion for building a business is also a great passion to have* and it well may be that the product or service is just incidental in that case.

3. The friend or neighbor dream killer:

Not only does everyone love to be asked for their advice but even more they love to give it. When you buy a new car or get a job promotion or have big news, you love to share it with friends and neighbors; that's why they are family and friends. Unfortunately, telling others what we do seems to automatically provide the right to give their advice even if they do not know anything about the subject. I'm always ready to give my opinion on anything! Just ask!

Answer: Without being rude or close minded, try to limit the input from well meaning, but non-expert people. If you are serious about starting you new business there may be value in not discussing it with some family or friends simply because you do not want to be burdened with the uninformed opinions of others.

4. The "Been there – done that" dream killer:

This one's real simple. You are bound to know family, friends or work colleagues that considered business ownership and for whatever reason decided not to move forward with it. So when they hear of your plans to start a new business they like nothing more than explaining in great detail why you shouldn't.

Answer: Focus on YOUR goals, and tune out uninformed or ill reasoned advice, whatever the source. It does not matter whether the person who is trying to hold you back is doing it for the right reasons or not. All that matters is if the advice is accurate and solid. If it is, then pay attention to it.

5. The "cold feet" dream killer:

This is probably the most common dream killer, and unfortunately, is self inflicted as we do it to ourselves. Starting a business is probably one of the three biggest decisions we make in life next to choosing a spouse and buying your first house. If you have a spouse or have at least bought one home you can remember the thought you gave and how it was a little bit scary. Deciding to go into business is a big thing, and it is definitely scary. So what can happen is that we set up a way to avoid that hard and scary decision by finding reasons to justify *not* going into business. We allow our fears to get ahead of our hopes. We deprive ourselves of the opportunity to achieve the very thing we most want...the independence, security and freedom that comes with being the boss of a successful business.

Answer: We must embrace being scared and use the fear factor to our advantage by letting it add an extra element of caution and care to our research. After you have clearly set your goals through your business plan, you must compare several different opportunities to each other to see which one most closely matches your "perfect business model."

6. The "sample of one" dream killer:

Too often potential business owners get feedback from one person about a particular business and make all future decisions on that one piece of feedback. Advice from just one person is always dangerous, and unfortunately this one works in both directions. For example, you may talk with someone who failed in that business or worse yet, just in the particular industry. As a result the potential business owner concludes the business is not for them - a rash conclusion. And conversely, the potential business owner hears one single success story and decides this is the business for them. Another rash conclusion!

Answer: A "sample of one" is always dangerous as it is too general. Also, it should not be attempted until you have a solid core of data collected over time from many reliable sources. Bottom line, check multiple opinions from multiple sources and take care to ask the same questions the same way so you get a complete picture. Don't ask multiple people a different set of questions as you have no true basis for comparison whether your final decision is positive or negative about the business, and whether it is a good "fit".

7. The "wrong set of questions" dream killer:

Often new business owners destroy their own dreams of business ownership by confusing casual inquiry with real research. For example, you may be considering a retail business and may try to find how many similar businesses are listed in the Yellow Pages. That's an interesting idea or data point but it doesn't indicate the real size of that market. If it's a business in a niche market, you need to know the proximity of each business to each other etc as it may well be that market in that area is under-served!

Answer: You must do your own research about the national, regional and local economy, the industry and the specific business you're planning to start. This is probably the hardest part for a new business owner starting out. You need to speak to as many of them as you can to get as many opinions as you can. If you can find a similar business in another location, speak to the owner to see if they are willing to share ideas with you. It may be, if you are not a direct competitive threat, that you could work together, share business plans and sales and marketing ideas, buy collectively and thereby getting better wholesale prices, build employee manuals and training manuals etc.

8. Paralysis by analysis:

Another form of dream killer, this describes people who never make a decision because their research never ends. Clear and detailed personal due diligence on any business opportunity is a must. Seek out *qualified* advice; but make sure it's qualified. Of course, talk to others in the same type of business that you are contemplating. Seek out attorneys, CPA's, and other qualified business experts but stay away from "expert opinions" from people who are not experts. There comes a time, however, when you have done enough research. It is time to make up your mind and make a decision. Acknowledge that research cannot answer every question. Some questions cannot be answered until you actually commit to a business, start doing it and then learn what the market has to tell you.

Answer: Clearly focus on your goals as you built them in your business plan and researched them and have faith in your own judgment. These are the best tools to avoid the indecision that comes from over analysis.

Conclusion:

After you have done all of them, review the data, and ask yourself these questions:
1. Do I still want to go into business for myself?
2. Have I discovered what it takes to be successful in this business, in terms of others who have already done this business, and in terms of opportunity in my marketplace?
    a. If so, do I fit the business?
    b. Am I like the people who have already succeeded in it?
    c. Do I know what the successful owner does?
    d. Can I do, or learn to do, what the successful owner does?
    e. Do I want to do what the successful owner does?
3. Assuming I succeed in this business, will it allow me to reach the personal, professional and family goals that I need from my business?
4. Is this the best business I have found to help me achieve my goals?

If the answer to all the above questions is "yes," then move forward with your goal of starting your business. If the answer to even a single one is "no," then it is not the business for you. Only if the answer is "I don't know," should you do more research. Knowledge of yourself, your goals, and your priorities is critical to making a good decision.

Passion - Good Or Bad?

As a Business Broker I keep hearing buyers or new business owners starting out reacting to something they have been told by family or well-meaning friends, and this is, if you intend going into business ownership make sure you: "Find your passion!" Focus on what you're passionate about and your likelihood of success increases.

I have thought a lot about "passion" and here's what I've come up with: After a short period of time the passion we had for something starts to slide. We need to look no further for this than our spouse, significant other or even our immediate family and friends. To re-invigorate these critical relationships that sustain us through life, we celebrate birthdays, anniversaries, and special occasions such as Thanksgiving and Christmas, other important events such as Easter or July 4th, plus ones that are important to us individually, such as graduation from college etc.

So this lack of passion we often experience in life with the job we have been doing leads us to think "There must be more." That is when we start to think 'Let me start a business of my own and do it my way."

Roadblock or Reality?

If that's the place in life where you are at, my advice to you would be "Don't dwell on passion or it will become a roadblock for you." And here's why. There are so many different types of businesses you can start. In the end your decision will boil down to three main things which all come together in one final question. The three things are:
1) How much money do you have to invest to start your business?
2) What lifestyle do you want this business to create for you?
3) Do you have the self belief that you have the skill to be successful?

If your answers to all three are yes, then your final question will be: When I weigh these three things together, do I feel ready to take the financial AND emotional risk? Taking the financial risk is both an emotional and logical decision, however taking the emotional risk is probably the hardest because there is no logic to it. Questions race through your mind such as "What will I do if I fail? What will I tell my family and friends if I fail? What will I do next? What will I tell the employees or ...? How will I recover from that lost money? How will I repay any debts I may have?"

So passion is nice but it's not critical. Consider some current business owners. There is the restaurant owner who has to multi task with food, employees, customers and a landlord. There is the hair salon owner who has to multitask with the different hair styles, employees, customers and landlord. There is the auto mechanic that has to multitask with the different make and models of cars, employees, customers and landlord.

I'm sure you get the point. Again, passion is good but not what this is all about. It's all about living your life with passion with your family, friends, and things that are important to you (lifestyle), by finding the right business that will provide the means for you to do that.

Passion is more about what you are being (**<u>business owner</u>**), than it is about what you are doing.

End Of Chapter Notes

Use this page to write down notes, ideas and other brainstorming for starting your business.

Section Two

Education

"*Be curious always! For knowledge will not acquire you: you must acquire it.*"

Dr. John G. Hibben

Introduction

The purpose of Section Two is to introduce some of the core and peripheral topics all business owners need to deal with when starting their business. I also suspect, almost without exception, areas we would prefer not to have to deal with as these topics are generally not part of our core competency and take more time to complete than we first thought. The topics I am referring to include topics such as the ethics and culture we create in our business, legal entity options and their importance, insurance options, some financial planning tools such as a start-up expense planner, sales forecast, personal budget planner, tax planning and lots of relevant subjects that require addressing to get a business successfully up and running.

The Perfect Business

As you build your business, make all your decisions on the basis that it is always for sale. This will drive the disciplines you need to be successful. Also, if you find an interested buyer your business and you are ready to go.

The perfect business is one with the following attributes:
1. A reasonable price
2. A reasonable down payment (hopefully about 30% of the full price)
3. Some seller financing
4. Reasonable sales (hopefully increasing each year)
5. Discretionary Earnings of $60,000 per annum or more
6. A compelling reason for sale
7. A desired industry type
8. Good and attractive location (if important for the business type)

Leadership

If it's your decision to start the business it will be your responsibility to make all major ongoing decisions. It's as simple as that. Welcome to Leadership.

From my experience, if you want to grow your business so it can be sold, you won't be able to retain the caliber of employees you need and have them stay, unless they feel part of the decision making process and engaged in the operation of the business.

Let's briefly look at five key traits of a leader:

Trait One: Vision
Not only do you own the vision but you own how it's communicated. Leadership is very esoteric but as a leader this is one of the skills you'll need to learn. Living, breathing, dreaming and being the vision of the business every day is what you will be about. Learn to inspire and touch by painting pictures with words. To see if you are successful, ask for feedback from those around – in particular those in the business environment. Your family and friends will probably tell you what you want to hear. Hearing first hand from an honest employee is much more important.

Trait Two: Integrity
What do you stand for? Whatever it is it will be seen and amplified by others, whether you like it or not. The law of attraction says we will attract those to us who are like us. If you make promises and don't follow through, or have no problem in exaggerating or distorting things, then when the pressure is on, that's what will be done and remembered. If, however you act with integrity and honesty that too will be remembered and copied by those around you.

Trait Three: Enthusiasm
A quote from Dale Carnegie says "Flaming enthusiasm, backed up by horse sense and persistence, is the quality that most frequently makes for success." I don't think this point needs to be any more complicated than that. If you bring enthusiasm to whatever you do, the rest will take care of itself.

Trait Four: Vital and clear thinking
I've thrown two of these into one as I think they go hand in hand. A leader has the ability to make clear and strong decisions – hearing all the arguments and then in a logical and unemotional way arrive at the right decision in the moment and then moving on. Good leaders know they have to make a decision in the moment and move forward. They also know that decisions can be over analyzed with 20/20 hindsight. But that's not an option for the leader. It's about the future not the past.

Trait Five: Team builder
A business that's attractive to a buyer is one that has future growth. A business that's much more attractive to a buyer is a business with future growth and the team already in place to deliver. A poor leader makes them the center of the business. A strong leader empowers those around them knowing that the leader is available if needed, otherwise good decisions have and will continue to be made by the quality of the team the leader has managed to assemble.

Ethics And Culture

Starting a business from scratch so it's ready for a buyer to buy is not a short term proposition. At a minimum I would suggest it's a three year plan with two at the absolute minimum and only in certain industries such as technology. Other businesses take time to understand what they can offer that makes them different in the market, build the systems, train the employees, create happy customers who help grow the business through positive word of mouth, while keeping suppliers and other support players happy and on board with the risks being taken.

This is an important point to remember as you work through your decision making process as the bottom line is that it's all about creating strong foundations. One of the short cuts to creating strong foundations is for the business to foster a work environment with strong, not negotiable ethics and a positive culture that doesn't require customers, employees, suppliers, creditors and others that come in contact with the business asking what the business is about, or more importantly about what it stands for. From my perspective, today's business environment demands honesty, trust, responsibility and other positive traits. If we make this part of the ethics and culture of our business, in my opinion it will allow for quicker growth, prosperity and success.

To illustrate the above, one of my work experiences was working at a Hewlett Packard site during the decision of HP to merge with Compaq. This was a merger of one extremely large global business (HP) with another very large competitor (Compaq.) A lot of the employees at Compaq had been in a previous merger and so had a different dynamic to a lot of the HP employees. What ensued was a clash of the different cultures making the work environment of the now combined HP/Compaq business a stressful, confusing and frustrating place to work until all the issues were addressed and everyone was able to re-focus.

The bottom line is that a workplace with the same ethics and culture that everyone understands and is a part of is, the goal. It saves wasting time and energy explaining this each and every time to customers, suppliers, new employees, and others. If it's set in stone early and everyone lives and breathes it, the results are the business success will be enhanced. If it's positive, then the results will be positive. If it's negative, the results will be negative.

Write down your ideas on what you would like to have in the Code of Ethics for your business.

Vision Statement/ Mission Statement/Confidentiality Policy/Privacy Policy

One of the ways to clearly communicate the reason for the business is through a Vision Statement and a Mission Statement. Both would appear prominently in your business and give clear direction and meaning to what your business stands for. A vision statement normally says where the business is going, while the Mission Statement states the purpose and values of the business.

Write down your ideas on what you would like to have in the Vision Statement for your business.

As mentioned above, a Code of ethics is about the behavior and conduct you would like your business and its employees known for.

Write down your ideas on what you would like to have in the Mission Statement for your business.

A confidentiality policy says how documents and information will be handled. This not only includes information about customers but also employees, suppliers, lenders and others that come in contact with the business. Why take the time and energy to have a Confidentiality Policy? Simple – it's part of your ethics and culture. If it's written down AND followed, no one has to ask what happens if ....

Write down your ideas on what you would like to have in the Confidentiality Policy of your business.

A Privacy Policy is not much different to a Confidentiality Policy. You can skip this one if you want or you can go with it so it's done and further reflects your ethics and culture. A Privacy Policy is about behavior, whereas a Confidentiality Policy is about what happens to sensitive material you get and what you will do with it.

Write down your ideas on what you would like to have in the Privacy of your business.

Legal Entity Options

As you move forward with getting ready to start your business, an important decision to make is the best form of legal entity. Your final decision does not mean you cannot change your mind or move from one entity to the other at a later stage. However, if you change entity it will incur costs from working directly with your accountant and/or attorney as well as any government filing fees.

If you want to file your own legal entity, you can do this yourself but if you want the right advice and the best information for your specific situation at a minimum, consult with an attorney, and if you are concerned about tax consequences, first consult with your accountant.

The following is a brief overview of the different legal entities:

Sole Proprietor

As a sole proprietor you will be responsible for all liabilities and debts in a business, so this is your legal exposure as the law views a sole proprietor and the business essentially as one and the same. You will also receive the profits and assets generated by the business so this is your financial exposure. A sole proprietor is the simplest type of business entity with all profits reported as personal income and taxed at your personal tax rates so this is your tax exposure. This can be a disadvantage once the business gets established and starts to generate a high level of profit and where you will need the services of a good accountant or tax agent. And remember, profit does not equal cash flow. You can be making a lot of money that attracts high taxes but be cash poor because all your profits are sitting in your business as accounts receivable.

The good news for using a Sole Proprietor as your legal entity is that there are no filing fees to either the Federal or State governments.

Partnership

A common way to spread risk, bring together two or more like-minded people, or create an entity that allows a number of people to come together with complimentary skill sets and/or interests, is through a partnership. As partners you share ownership of a business by spreading around the downside or risks, based on each person's capital infusions. You also share the upside which is the profits of the business or its gain when the business is sold. To protect all partners in the business, you need to have a legal agreement drafted that defines the division of profits and assets, how much each partner will contribute in capital, how disputes will be resolved, provisions for adding additional partners, and how the business should be dissolved or bought out by a partner.

A legal agreement is important because, like any relationship, not all business partners are good matches and the situation could eventually change. Similar to Sole Proprietors, partners and the business itself are viewed as one entity by the law. There are three types of partnerships:

General Partnership: A joint venture that is typically shared equally (unless otherwise stated in the legal agreement), with equal division of profits, losses and responsibilities.

Limited Partnership: This form of partnership generally specifies that the participants have limited liability and also limits the input to management decisions. This structure may not work well for service or retail businesses and is best used for bringing in investors for short term projects.

Joint Venture: This structure is used for a short term investment or project. If the partners continue working together on an ongoing basis, the structure must be changed to one of the other options.

Final thought

Is a partnership a good business option? The honest answer is that it is a good business option but that it has the highest probability of not working out. A lot of businesses close down for different reasons and these can include partner disputes, frustration at not being able to achieve what brought the partners together in the first place, or the partners not realizing that they thought they were just bringing a partner into the business, not his spouse and children, who have their own demands and dynamic.

Corporation

Corporations came into existence to provide legal protection for the owners of the business and to allow an interest in the business to be sold in exchange for an investor putting in capital that generated a return on that investment. An interest in the business is also known as a share. A corporation is its own entity that is taxed, can be sued, and can enter into contractual agreements in its own right. The owners of a corporation are shareholders who elect a board of directors to oversee the major decisions and policies of the company. Since the corporation is its own entity, it can continue even when ownership changes hands. Shareholders in corporations have less liability than sole proprietors, however, officers of the company can be held liable for legal matters such as failing to pay taxes or payroll. Corporations can deduct the cost of benefits for employees, officers and as we said above, can raise capital by selling shares of the company stock.

Incorporating requires a significant amount of paperwork and corporations must comply with federal, state, and some local agencies. Dividends that are paid to shareholders are not deductible as business income, which can result in paying higher taxes. This is also known as a C Corporation.

Creating a corporation is usually done in your home state but you can incorporate in another US state that doesn't have fees nor tax the profits of out-of-state income, also called a foreign corporation. Keep in mind, if you do incorporate somewhere other than your home state, you may have to pay additional fees and meet additional requirements. For the full understanding of all the options, you may want to speak with an accountant or tax advisor before making a final decision.

Because Corporations are an effective legal and tax entity, it was decided to make this option available to individuals including families and this is known as the S Corp.

Subchapter "S" Corporation

This is a tax election that allows a shareholder to treat profits as distributions and pass through to his or her personal tax return. This means that the shareholder must be paid a salary that meets the standards of "reasonable compensation" – meaning that the wages are comparable to what would be paid to someone in a similar position. If this is not done, the IRS can reclassify the business and require the shareholder to pay taxes on all of the profits and earnings.

Limited Liability Company (LLC)

A Limited Liability Company is a relatively new structure that bridges the gap between a general partnership and a corporation, bringing together the protection from personal liability offered by corporations and the flexibility of a partnership. The duration of a LLC is determined when the business is filed, though it can be extended if members agree. LLC's must not have more than two of the four characteristics that define corporations: limited liability to the extent of assets; continuity of life; centralization of management; and free transferability of ownership interests. Federal tax forms for LLC's are typically the same as the forms used for partnerships. However, if more than two of the characteristics that define a corporation exist, the business must file corporation forms.

Given the complexities, legal and tax ramifications and benefits of each business structure, it is important to consult with your accountant and/or attorney to get the best advice on your particular situation.

If you would like to do some additional research before meeting with your accountant or attorney, go the IRS website at www.irs.gov

Federal Income Tax:

The method of paying federal income tax depends on your legal form of business. The following apply for the different entities:

Sole Proprietorship:

Federal income tax for a Sole Proprietor is made with your Schedule C tax return and part of your Form 1040 Federal Income Tax return.

Partnership:

A Federal Partnership return is filed or Form 1065. This is an informational return that shows gross and net earnings of profit and loss which flows to the individuals earnings of each partner when they complete and report their individual return on Form 1040.

Corporation:

Corporations must file an 1120 tax return for the entity in its own right. Any earnings from the corporation including salary and other income such as dividends are then reported on your personal federal individual return on Form 1040.

Federal Payroll Tax:

If a business employs a person they must register with the IRS and acquire an Employer Identification Number and pay federal withholding tax at least quarterly.

Fictitious Business Name Or DBA

Once you have decided on your legal entity it may be necessary to create a Fictitious Business Name or Doing Business As (DBA)

Your reason for creating and filing a Fictitious Business Name depends on the legal entity you have chosen. For example, if you have decided to operate as a sole proprietor the only name you can really use when you market yourself is your name. This may not suit you as you may want to sound like a large company or your personal name doesn't reflect the service you provide. For example, if your business is cutting hair and your name is Bill Smith, that doesn't sound like a good business name to use. Hair Cuts for All or $10 Hair Cuts or Elite Hair Salon has much different appeal.

Conversely, you may have chosen to incorporate, and plan on having multiple locations with different names, for example, a series of bars. One name could be Sacramento Bar and Grill, one could be Reno Bar and Grill and one could be New York's Finest Bar and Grille. Guess where they are located?

In some U.S. states you register your assumed name with the Secretary of State or other state agency, but in most states, registration is handled at the county level, and each county may have different forms and fees for registering a name. Generally speaking, the process is fairly simple: you perform a search through their database to make sure the name is not already in use, then submit a simple form, along with the correct filing fee (anywhere from $10 to $50). Some states also require that you publish a notice in your local newspaper and submit an affidavit to show that you have fulfilled the publication requirement. Call your county clerk's office to find out the local fees and procedures in your area.

Use the template below to brainstorm some business names that reflect the image and character of the business you are going to open.

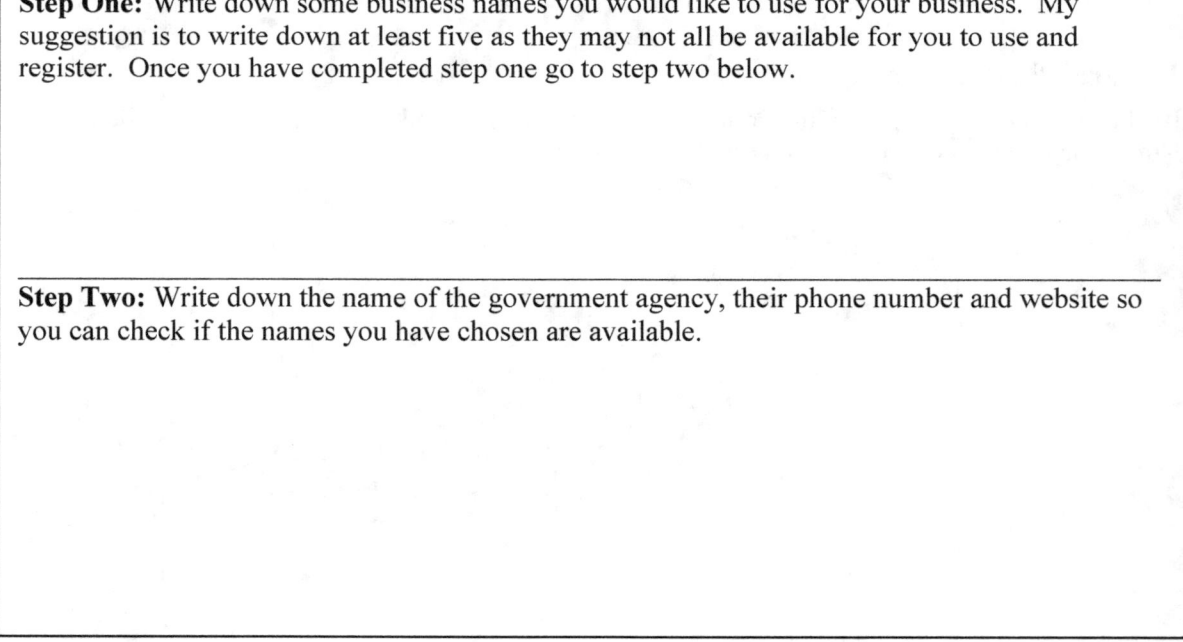

Step One: Write down some business names you would like to use for your business. My suggestion is to write down at least five as they may not all be available for you to use and register. Once you have completed step one go to step two below.

_____

Step Two: Write down the name of the government agency, their phone number and website so you can check if the names you have chosen are available.

Federal Employer Identification Number

Each business operating in the United States needs a valid Employer Identification Number (EIN). It's like a Social Security Number for a business and is used for tax reporting purposes. An EIN is required if you have one or more employees on a payroll, or if you have chosen to create a corporation or partnership. If your business has started its life as a sole proprietorship and you don't do certain types of business activities you are not required to apply for an EIN. However, if you are concerned about sending your Social Security number to businesses asking for your EIN, you can apply for an EIN to the IRS.

For more information about EIN's and lots of other good business information, go to the IRS website http://www.irs.gov and work your way down through the Businesses tab or do a search for what you need. I did not include URL's to specific sites within the IRS as the pages may get updated or changed and thereby superseding the URL.

Another excellent site for business information is the US government site: http://www.business.gov

Business License And Other Licenses And Permits

Every state, city, and county has different regulations for general business licenses. A business license allows you to comply with your area business requirements. The fees range from $50 to $300 and are renewed each year.

Certain types of businesses may also be required to apply for special business licenses. For example, businesses dealing with alcoholic beverages, firearms, used goods or adult entertainment may require special license approval. Some businesses may require a permit issued by the local sheriff or other enforcement agency. Make sure you are aware of these requirements as you may have to pay a fine or in the worst case, close down and be prohibited from opening again. These licenses can also take longer to be issued, sometimes up to three months, so be sure to apply early.

The other license to be aware of is a Contractor's License. A lot of states regulate the minimum education and experience standards for contractors to perform work. In California, all regulations are the responsibility of the Contractors State License Board. Check your state government to see if you have similar requirements if you are planning on starting your business in one of these industries. The websites below may be able to assist you. Please be aware the links may change so if this happens, go to the home page of the website and do a search for "business license."

Business License Resources by State

- ✓ Alabama – www.ador.state.al.us/licenses/authrity/html
- ✓ Alaska – www.dced.state.ak.us/occ/buslic.htm
- ✓ Arizona – www.revenue.state.az.us/license.htm
- ✓ Arkansas – www.state.ar.us/online_business.php
- ✓ California – www.calgold.ca.gov/
- ✓ Colorado – www.state.co.us/gov_dir/obd/blid.htm
- ✓ Connecticut – www.state.ct.us/
- ✓ Delaware – www.state.de.us/revenue/obt/obtmain.htm
- ✓ District of Columbia – www.dcra.dc.gov/
- ✓ Florida – http://sun6.dms.state.fl.us/dor/businesses/

- ✓ Georgia – www.sos.state.ga.us/corporations/regforms.htm
- ✓ Hawaii – www.hawaii.gov/dbedt/start/starting.html
- ✓ Idaho – www.idoc.state.id.us/Pages/BUSINESSPAGE.html
- ✓ Illinois – www.sos.state.il.us/departments/business_services/business.html
- ✓ Indiana – www.state.in.us/sic/owners/ia.html
- ✓ Iowa – www.iowasmart.com/blic/
- ✓ Kansas – www.accesskansas.org/businesscenter/index.html?link=start
- ✓ Kentucky – www.thinkkentucky.com/kyedc/ebpermits.asp
- ✓ Louisiana – www.sec.state.la.us/comm/fss/fss-index.htm
- ✓ Maine – www.econdevmaine.com/biz-develop.htm
- ✓ Maryland – www.dllr.state.md.us/
- ✓ Massachusetts – www.state.ma.us/sec/cor/coridx.htm
- ✓ Michigan – http://medc.michigan.org/services/startups/index2.asp
- ✓ Minnesota – www.dted.state.mn.uss
- ✓ Mississippi – www.olemiss.edu/depts/mssbdc/going_intobus.html
- ✓ Missouri – www.ded.state.mo.us/business/businesscenter/
- ✓ Montana – www.state.mt.us/sos/biz/htm
- ✓ Nebraska – www.nebraska.gov/business/html/337/index.phtml
- ✓ New Hampshire – www.nhsbdc.org/startup.htm
- ✓ New Jersey – www.state.nj.us/njbiz/s_lic_and_cert.shtml
- ✓ New Mexico – http://edd.state.nm.us/NMBUSINESS/
- ✓ Nevada – www.nv.gov
- ✓ North Carolina – www.secstate.state.nc.us/secstate/blio/default.htm
- ✓ North Dakota – www.state.nd.us/sec/
- ✓ Ohio – www.state.oh.us/sos/business_services_information.htm
- ✓ Oklahoma – www.okonestop.com/
- ✓ Oregon – www.filinginoregon.com
- ✓ Pennsylvania – www.paopenforbusiness.state.pa.us
- ✓ Rhode Island – www.corps.state.ri.us/firststop/index.asp
- ✓ South Carolina – www.state.sd.us/STATE/sitecategory.cfm?mp=Licenses/Occupations
- ✓ South Dakota - www.sd.gov/Main_Login.asp
- ✓ Tennessee – www.state.tn.us/ecd/res_guide.htm
- ✓ Texas – www.tded.state.tx.us/guide/
- ✓ Utah – www.commerce.state.ut.us/web/commerce/admin/licen.htm
- ✓ Vermont – www.sec.state.vt.us/
- ✓ Virginia – www.dba.state.va.us/
- ✓ Washington – www.wa.gov/dol/bpd/limsnet.htm
- ✓ West Virginia – www.state.wv.us/taxrev//busreg.html
- ✓ Wisconsin – www.wdfi.org/corporations/forms/
- ✓ Wyoming – http://soswy.state.wy.us/corporat/corporat.htm

Additional Resources:
- ✓ The IRS also offers links to every state with multiple business resources:
  www.irs.gov/businesses/small/article/0,,id=99021,00.html

- ✓ Business.gov provides legal and regulatory information to small businesses in the U.S. This site is loaded with excellent information for every state to help entrepreneurs find answers and resolve problems and can be found at:
  www.Business.gov.

Sales And Use Taxes

At a national level there is currently no sales tax levied or paid on any goods and services. However, at a state level this sort of tax does apply except for the states of Alaska, Delaware, Montana, New Hampshire and Oregon. If your business sells taxable goods and you are in a state in the US that collects sales tax, you will need to apply for a resale license. A resale license or Sales Tax Exemption Certificate will be needed if you purchase from wholesalers, allowing you to buy your merchandise without paying sales tax. This also means that you are responsible for collecting taxes when you make a sale. Each state and local authority has different requirements for tax rates, collection and reporting methods. The Business Owner's Tool Kit website has an excellent directory of tax requirements for each state: www.toolkit.cch.com/text/P07_4500.asp

Insurance Options

When the subject of insurance comes up we tend to want to run and hide as it's something we hope we don't need. Plus it can get pretty complicated trying to understand all the variables, decide your risk comfort and when it's all said and done, how much you can afford to pay. There are different insurance policies for different reasons. The main policies you may wish to consider starting out with for your business are below. However, as you explore the different insurance options, the insurance companies you contact will be glad to advise you on what you are inquiring about and make suggestions on what they believe you will need.

Use the templates at the end of this topic to do some comparison shopping and get this task accomplished…until renewal time in 12 months.

Liability Insurance or General Business Insurance

General Business Insurance or Liability Insurance protects you from lawsuits filed for accidents, injuries and negligence. Also, under this policy, if you are ever the target of a frivolous lawsuit, your insurance policy should take care of the legal fees and litigations. Not all policies are created equal, however, so be sure to check the details of any policy that you consider.

If you are going to lease a commercial location for your business, your landlord will probably require proof of liability insurance. Since the fees for this type of insurance can vary, it is a good idea to get some quotes early on and build this expense into your budget.

Business Interruption

If your business ceases to operate due to a fire or some other form of accident there are taxes, utilities and other continuing expenses to pay until the building is rebuilt and you can recommence trading. Business Interruption insurance provides money to pay fixed expenses until you are operational again.

Commercial Property Insurance

In the event of a disaster from fire, smoke, hail or wind the commercial property could be damaged. Coverage also extends to vandalism and civil disobedience. If you are renting the building, the property owner probably carries some level of insurance. You should ask what is covered in his policy. When in doubt, it is always best to carry your own policy.

Worker's Compensation Insurance

Many states now require that companies with employees carry worker's compensation insurance. This type of policy covers damages resulting from employee injuries. It is relatively expensive in some states (like California) so it would be wise to factor this into your plan early. Check the state listings provided in this chapter to find out if your area requires that you carry worker's comp insurance.

Commercial Auto Insurance

If you have a company vehicle or a business that makes deliveries, you will need a commercial auto policy. These policies can include coverage for collisions, comprehensive, rental cars, and towing. Also check your existing coverage of vehicles for both you and your employees (if applicable), since personal auto insurance does not always cover claims that occur during business operation.

Professional Liability Insurance

If your business is providing services, you should consider having professional liability insurance (also known as errors and omissions insurance). This type of liability coverage protects your business against malpractice, errors, negligence in provision of services to your customers. Depending on your profession, you may be required by your state government to carry such a policy. For example, physicians are required to purchase malpractice insurance as a condition of practicing in certain states.

Life Insurance

If you are the main bread winner in your family or you have debts that need to be paid, then life insurance is the means to protect your loved ones. With a good life insurance policy, if you should be accidentally killed then the insurance policy will pay off both your personal and business debts if the correct amount of coverage is in place. Check into this one thoroughly as debt can cripple a family and for a relatively small monthly premium provide a lot of peace and mind.

Key Man Insurance

This policy is complimentary to Life Insurance mentioned above. If you (and/or any other individual) are so critical to the operation of your business that it cannot continue in the event of your illness or death, you should consider "key man" insurance. This type of policy is frequently required by banks or government loan programs. It also can be used to provide continuity in operations during a period of ownership transition caused by the death or incapacitation of an owner or other "key" employee.

Officer and Director

Under most state laws, officers and directors of a corporation may become personally liable for their actions on behalf of the company. This type of policy covers this liability.

Home-Based Business Insurance

Contrary to popular belief, homeowners' insurance policies do not generally cover home-based business losses. Depending on risks to your business, you may add riders to your homeowners' policy to cover normal business risks such as property damage. However, homeowners policies only go so far and you may need to buy additional cover for other risks, such as general and professional liability.

Where to Locate Insurance Providers

Contact the broker that handles your auto or home owner's insurance to find out if he also offers business insurance. If not, they should be able to refer you to someone who does. You can also visit www.InsuranceFinder.com for a list of resources by state or Google the web.

To help evaluate different policies from different insurance companies, the following may help.

Insurance company name:	
Name of Agent:	
Contact number:	
Coverage key points including amount	
Premium quoted:	
Notes:	

Insurance company name:	
Name of Agent:	
Contact number:	
Coverage key points including amount	
Premium quoted:	
Notes:	

Insurance company name:	
Name of Agent:	
Contact number:	
Coverage key points including amount	
Premium quoted:	
Notes:	

Insurance company name:	
Name of Agent:	
Contact number:	
Coverage key points including amount	
Premium quoted:	
Notes:	

Insurance company name:	
Name of Agent:	
Contact number:	
Coverage key points including amount	
Premium quoted:	
Notes:	

Insurance company name:	
Name of Agent:	
Contact number:	
Coverage key points including amount	
Premium quoted:	
Notes:	

Operations Manual

An operations manual is a must for every business. It serves as a great help to each new hire who joins your business, plus it is invaluable as a training tool for your current employees. Plus here are some great benefits you may not have considered:

1. Creating an operations manual allows you to set standards and define benchmarks that become the standard in the business. For example, and very simply, all phones must be answered within 3 rings, all email must be acknowledged within 48 hours, all times must use the time clock to record when they start and finish…and so it goes on.
2. Don't write the operations manual yourself, have this done by you or more of your key employees.
3. Part of the reason for two above is that you don't have time but the other reason is that if you get your team to write the operations manual it shows you what they do and don't know. But here's the best part, you can spot check the operations manual whenever you have a moment, when something is done below standard, you have a new hire that asks how something is done. If you can't find the answer or the answer you see written down is not acceptable to you, it's time to bring the team together and do a training session.
4. Or – and this is the great or – team members should be bringing items to you for determination on best practice or how something should be done. If you're a good manager your answer should be to not accept the question being asked of you but ask the bringer of the question what he thinks the answer should be. Does this mean the group will avoid bringing you questions – maybe – but if they own the operations manual and you don't have a problem with a solution in the operations manual, whose responsibility is that? Your teams? Yes – it's your business but running the business effectively on a day to day basis is their responsibility.

If focus and energy is truly applied to the operations manual, it should uncover a number of areas for initial and then ongoing discussion. Creating an effective operations manual is a continuous work in progress. So is creating the business culture that recognizes its importance. Michael Gerber, the author of the E Myth and the E Myth Revisited is an expert on this subject. Buy his books and get some great insights.

You will also find that you learn quite a bit about your business when you put your manual together because it forces you to consider all aspects of your business operations. You may want to have an online version and a version that is printed and placed in a binder for easy access. And as we've said, your manual can also empower your employees to run your business when you're not there.

When writing your manual, choose the best writer on the team AND the person who gets on well with as many of your team as possible. A great writer who doesn't like interacting with the employees is not a good mix. Try to cover as much as possible while keeping the instructions simple. Think about a typical day and what needs to happen throughout the day for each position. Start by outlining the tasks of a typical day. Write in a conversational style and explain procedures in a step-by-step format. Make sure all of the directions are clear and that it doesn't leave the reader confused or with unanswered questions. When you have a finished draft, ask employees to read it and give you feedback. After this is done, test as much as you can by having a member of the team who normally doesn't do that task, attempt the task by following what's in the operations manual. This is the place that things really happen as I guarantee pieces will not be clear and there will be a lot of frustration. Manage it carefully as part of the truth is that the employees with the knowledge don't like giving it up. If somebody else can do their job they lose a bit of security by realizing that maybe they are disposable and this is not something they want to be reminded about.

Here are some topics to cover in your operations manual. It's best to create your manual using a word processing system so that you can save your work and make changes when necessary. And make sure you regularly back up this file. You'd hate to do put six months work into the operations manual and then lose it all to have to start all over again.

- ✓ Company Overview & History
- ✓ Mission Statement
- ✓ Opening Procedures
- ✓ Closing Procedures
- ✓ Cash Handling
- ✓ Daily Tasks
- ✓ Alarm System Operations
- ✓ Safe Opening and Closing Procedures
- ✓ Contact Numbers for Emergencies or Information
- ✓ Employee Shift Coverage
- ✓ Website Procedures
- ✓ Customer Service Procedures
- ✓ Sales Procedures
- ✓ Sales Quotas
- ✓ Commission Payments
- ✓ Order Processing
- ✓ Credit Card Processing
- ✓ Refunds and Returns
- ✓ Gift Certificates
- ✓ Special Orders
- ✓ Shipping & Receiving
- ✓ Equipment Handling
- ✓ Equipment Maintenance (replacing printer cartridges, receipt tape, etc.).
- ✓ Security Procedures
- ✓ Emergency Procedures
- ✓ Product Pricing and Discounts
- ✓ Other Miscellaneous Procedures and Anything Specific to the Way Your Business Operates

Organization Chart

An Organization chart or Org chart, is probably one of the simplest and most powerful tools to create, use and update, yet probably one of the most ignored by business owners.

Why is it so powerful? It's so powerful as it forces the business owner to decide what position is needed, who the position reports to, and the role of that position. If a business grows, it naturally requires new employees to handle the additional work. The Org chart is the starting point as it determines who the position reports to, a job description for each position, and an analysis to make sure all positions have the appropriately educated, trained, and skilled holder of that position.

The Org chart can also be used in sales presentations to show the structure of the business and showcase its dynamic. Software to create Org charts is easy to find. Search the web for a dedicated piece of software if that is your preference or products from Microsoft such as Word, PowerPoint and Visio can readily do the task for you. Do your Org chart now and make sure it's maintained as you go and kept in a common place so it's easily found. If you are a nostalgic person, frame your very first Org chart so you can look back on it in years to come to see how you've grown.

Job Descriptions

Probably the most important business decision you make is actually deciding to go into business. The next most important decision you make is each person you hire and bring into the business. Make the right decision and it brings success to the business. Make the wrong decision and it can become a total distraction for many reasons including lost revenue, lost time, low morale for the other employees, and lost opportunities for the business, to name a few reasons.

Your goal in hiring may have many reasons but it should have one purpose and one purpose only, and this is to find the brightest, most competent, flexible, reliable, multifaceted employee you can find at the best price possible for that position. This is not to suggest you find the cheapest person and exploit them as that simply will not work. But you must get a Return On your Investment otherwise you will not have a business because you have gone broke.

If the above makes sense, your goal is to create the best job description you can. Putting your employment needs down onto paper not only helps you clarify the work you want the new hire to do but also help them in the hiring process to be sure they have the skills you need and can fit the need you've identified. A job description also helps your recruiter if you outsource that service.

The goals of a good job description include:

- ✓ Helps you or the manager of the position and any other employees already performing the job to agree on the responsibilities and scope of the position,
- ✓ Helps you know the knowledge, skills, education, experience, and capabilities you seek in your new employee, so an effective recruiting plan is formulated,
- ✓ Informs candidates about the duties and responsibilities of the position for which they are applying.
- ✓ Informs employees who are assisting with the interview process about the questions to ask candidates and what you seek in the new employee.

✓ May protect you legally when you can demonstrate why the candidate selected for a position was your most qualified and culturally suited applicant.

The content of a good job description includes:

✓ **Title:** Job title of the position being advertised.
✓ **Accountability:** Who the applicant is accountable to.
✓ **Responsibility:** What the applicant is responsible for.
✓ **Location:** Where the applicant will be based.
✓ **Purpose of the job:** What the applicant is expected to achieve.
✓ **Main duties:** A brief description of the position defining the principle areas of responsibility.
✓ **Terms of employment:** Hours of work, salary scale, holiday entitlement.

Interview Techniques

If your business is small and you have decided to handle the job hiring responsibility yourself, make sure you read as much as you can so you don't ask irrelevant questions or inadvertently inappropriate questions. If you have not conducted job interviews before, consider having a staffing or employment hiring company such as Remedy Staffing, Volt or Select Personnel do this for you. If that doesn't feel right, have them come to your business and do the interviewing with you so you see how it's done and build the necessary skills. Hiring the right person is too important to guess; you have to get it right first time. Additionally, if you don't present well during the interview, you may find the perfect person but they decide not to join your business because they weren't comfortable with the interview etc.

Here are some suggestions as you move towards hiring a new person.

1. Build and document your processes – job description/interview questions for each position and don't vary them for each candidate. If you vary what you ask for different candidates you will not have a benchmark to compare each candidate.
2. Hire for today's need and tomorrow's vision.
3. Clearly understand the job you are filling.
4. Be legal.
5. Build and use a standardized hiring process.
6. Hire the right person – you want to make a profit from their employment or ROI.
7. Avoid hiring someone just because they are similar to you. Despite the best of intentions, interviewers and supervisors have an unconscious tendency to favor people who are similar to themselves.
8. Consider using your team to recruit – though rules and training are needed.

Employee Manual

A subject we discussed in this section was insurance. Whether or not you believe in insurance, an Employee Manual is another form of insurance as it can prevent you being sued by a disgruntled employee who felt harassed, passed over or not given enough protection from a customer, fellow worker or manager. An employee manual may sound like the domain of large corporations but it serves a very positive purpose for a number of reasons. These include a working document that is ready to go for a new employee from day one who wants to know and understand how the business works. Because it's a reference tool, once it is created it can easily be updated, so this provides great flexibility. Finally, if an issue does arise, by having a written document it does provide some protection if the decision you made was within the terms of the employee manual that was presented to the employee the day they joined the business.

Whether or not you need an employee manual is your decision, though it can take a lot of time keeping your policies consistent and up to date. You should have a manual like this reviewed by an attorney to make sure it is compliant with local and federal laws.

The following is a sample outline that you can use as a guideline for your manual. Simply drop the headings into some word processing software and fill it out. Alternatively, as I mentioned above, have your attorney put something together for you ...but don't ignore it.

1. INTRODUCTION
    1.1 Welcome
    1.2 History

2. EMPLOYMENT POLICIES
    2.1 Probationary Period for New Employees
    2.2 Equal Employment Opportunity
    2.3 Affirmative Action/Diversity
    2.4 Americans with Disabilities Act
    2.5 Immigration Law Compliance
    2.6 Employee Background Check
    2.7 Criminal Records
    2.8 New Employee Orientation
    2.9 Personnel Records and Administration
    2.10 Safety
    2.11 Building Security
    2.12 Personal Property
    2.13 Visitors in the Workplace

3. STANDARDS OF CONDUCT
    3.1 General Guidelines
    3.2 Attendance and Punctuality
    3.3 Absence and Lateness
    3.4 Sexual Harassment Policy
    3.5 Confidential Information and Nondisclosure
    3.6 Ethical Standards
    3.7 Dress Code
    3.8 Use of Computer, Phone and Mail
    3.9 Use of Internet
    3.10 Smoking Policy
    3.11 Employment Termination/Resignation

4 COMPENSATION POLICIES
    4.1 Base Compensation
    4.2 Performance Bonuses
    4.3 Overtime Pay
    4.4 Payroll and Paydays

Posters

Labor laws require certain posters be displayed for the employees to readily see during their work day. For more information go to: http://www.business.gov/guides/employment/managing/posters.html

Training Manual

I am personally a great believer in a training manual. The reasons why include:
1. If it's written down once it is easy to update and change, as change is inevitable. This is given as the number one reason NOT to create a training manual. My counter argument to that is that if things are changing that much, how do you communicate to everyone, in particular any new hires, the current method or process to follow.

2. For a training manual to be effective it must be in a central place so ALL employees have 24/7 access to it. This solution also contributes to solving number one above.
3. Michael Gerber, the author of The E Myth and The E Myth Revisited talks constantly about working on your business not in your business. An effective and proper training manual allows you to do that.
4. This is the best news for the business owner. This is not a task you own – this is a task you delegate to one of your employees. Choose somebody that has the respect of all your team, understands the power of a good training manual and has the enthusiasm to keep it current and communicate changes as necessary.
5. In an earlier topic in this section I talked about ethics and culture. An effective training manual is part of that culture as when anyone asks a question – how do I …? or what do I do if …? The first question from management should be – what does the training manual say to do? If the training manual is up to date, you have just created a method for the employee to solve his own problem so now he's empowered and you've prevented somebody being interrupted to answer a question so now that person is more productive. A pure win/win for everyone – especially the business.
6. A good training manual works in conjunction with a good operations manual and it is definitely appropriate for them to cross reference each other.
7. Plus – did I mention that an effective training manual is a great tool for new hires to learn your business?

Design:

Developing a training manual does take a lot of work. If your business can afford it then hire a technical writer to do this for you. They have the skill to break everything down logically, present it graphically and make the manual look professional with its presentation. There are also different approaches to creating an effective training manual that is beyond the scope of this guide. If hiring a technical writer is not an option, have the team agree on a format that works for the majority and move forward from there. One of the complaints will be that the manual is hard to follow. However, that can be a training exercise and then you move on.

A well-designed training manual, that is kept up to date, can become a valuable source of information to the organization. An effective manual:
✓ Is easy to read and has easy to follow instructions
✓ Has an attractive design
✓ Uses illustrations to enhance understanding
✓ Can be used for future reference

The following should be taken in consideration when designing the manual:
✓ Content – topics, tasks, procedures and other information arranged in a logical sequence and broken down into small units
✓ Audience – their reading skills, previous work experience
✓ How the manual is to be used during the training session, afterwards (for revision) and/or as a reference in the work place

Writing the manual

Writing the manual takes place in three steps. First, determine the purpose of the manual. Second, agree on a layout and design so you can build a draft. Third, write the manual by collecting all items of interest. Discard material or subjects as the documents evolve or make sure it's included because of its importance.

Consider the following:
- ✓ Write in plain English: Avoid using technical terms, unless it is part of the work place language. Use a glossary to explain the technical terms so new hires aren't intimidated and come back. Also, spell out or explain acronyms and abbreviations.
- ✓ Use the active voice as it concise, easier to read and shorter to write.
- ✓ Be consistent in the use of terminology, tone and style of writing. This will happen if there is one main writer, but if it gets done quicker and time is a priority, use other writers.
- ✓ Reader attention span has been challenged by the internet. We no longer like long sentences and paragraphs as they can be confusing. Use short sentences and phrases. Numbered steps are easier to follow than long paragraphs.
- ✓ Include illustrations (graphs, flow charts, tables, pictures, screen displays, examples of finished tasks) where appropriate, to clarify concepts and enhance understanding. It also adds visual interest. Illustrations should be in proper proportion to nearby text.
- ✓ Writing the manual will be so much easier in good software. Use a program that's widely used and it may already include a template you can model off, for example, Microsoft Word.
- ✓ Create a detailed table of contents that include chapter headings as well as the next level of subheadings or go back to the last comment and see if that works.
- ✓ Write a detailed index, including cross-references, to make it easy to find information. A good index makes the manual usable as a reference work for future use.
- ✓ Check spelling and grammar.

After the completion of the first draft get feedback from key employees and implement any suggestions. Try to gather as many opinions as practical as it allows input from everyone on the importance of the document and makes them feel they own the document including keeping it up to date. This last point is critical. Many employees will think it's a waste of time until they see it saves them time.

The name of the manual, author(s), company name, publishing date should be included. If items are confidential, this is not the place to write them down. You can reference them in the manual by pointing out who to contact for access to these documents. A copyright notice can be included, as well as acknowledgement of contributors, if appropriate.

Presentation

Try to make the manual as attractive and professional in appearance as possible. This gives the manual greater status. Even consider key employees carrying it to meetings to again denote its importance, even if it just sits on the table. The following may be helpful with presentation:
- ✓ Section dividers to make it easy to find sections.
- ✓ A detailed table of contents at the beginning of sections, in addition to the main table of contents at the front of the manual makes it more accessible.
- ✓ Allow good size margins to accommodate binding or copying as well as space for users to make key notes.
- ✓ When considering binding, use a method that would allow easy replacement of pages. The manual can be updated easily, which adds to its reference value.

Lastly, be aware of copyright and other legal issues before reproducing the manual.

Patents/Trademarks/Copyright

If your business will create Intellectual property then you may need guidance from a qualified attorney so you and your business are protected. Intellectual property normally covers the three areas of Patents, Trade Marks and Copyright. Below is a very high level summary of each of the three areas and where you can go for registration and more information.

Patents

A patent is a claim that you, as an inventor, have made something unique and so wish to protect it from use including commercial exploitation by others. A patent doesn't require you to do anything, it simply stops others from using your patent. The means to protect your invention is through applying for a U.S. patent. Because of the complexities, professional assistance from a patent attorney is strongly urged because patent procedures are detailed and technical. A patent search is performed to see if a patent currently exists on the same or nearly the same device and, if not, to make proper application with the Patent Office.

Note: Only attorneys and agents registered with the U.S. Patent Office may represent inventors in related matters. The office has geographical and alphabetical listings of the more than 11,000 registered agents. Only these agents may perform patent searches in the patent office. Inventors or their attorneys can make arrangements with one of those agents. U.S. patents are issued by the Assistant Commissioner of Patents, Washington, D.C.

Additional information is provided in the publication, General Information Concerning Patents and other publications distributed through the U.S. Patent and Trademark Office.

To register a patent, contact:
U.S. Patent & Trademark Office
Mail Stop: USPTO Contact Center
400 Dulany Street
P.O. Box 1450
Alexandria VA 22313-1450
(800) 786-9199
Asst. Commissioner for Trademarks, Patent Applications
Washington, D.C. 20231
(800) 786-9199
Also, visit their web site at: http://www/uspto.gov

Trade Marks

Trademarks are names or symbols used in any commerce that is subject to regulation by state government or the U.S. Congress.

State Registration of a Trademark:

Trademarks and service marks may be registered in a state for a term of ten years. For more information about Applications for Registration of Trademark or Service Mark in your state, contact your state government.

Federal Registration of Trademark and Patent

To register a trademark federally contact:

U.S. Patent & Trademark Office

Mail Stop: USPTO Contact Center

400 Dulany Street

P.O. Box 1450

Alexandria VA 22313-1450

(800) 786-9199

Also, visit their web site at: http://www/uspto.gov

Caution: Federally registered trademarks may conflict with and supersede state registered business and product names. Businesses are encouraged to check for conflicts with federal trademarks.

Copyrights

Copyrights protect the thoughts and ideas of authors, composers and artists. A copyright prevents illegal copying of written matter, works of art or computer programs. In order to ensure copyright protection, the copyright owner should always include notices on all copies of the work.

Contact:
U.S. Library of Congress
James Madison Memorial Building
Washington, D.C. 20559
(202) 707 9100 Order Line
(202) 707 3000 Information Line

For more information:

http://www.uspto.gov This is the United States Patent and Trade Mark Organization.

http://www.stopfakes.gov/sf_how.asp#category1

http://www.sba.gov/index.html and then use the search feature for "patent" or "trade mark" or "copyright."

Finance Planning Tools

The axiom goes: If you can't measure it you cannot manage it. And so it is with the importance of making financial tracking tools, such as a cash flow forecast or pro forma for the business, and just as importantly, your personal life.

Starting a business means you will be taking on risk as you plan, open, and get your business functioning, and part of the economy. In Section Four we talk about the 7 stages of the business life cycle. However, our immediate goal in this topic is to build some financial planning tools that will tell you where you need to be to start the venture but more importantly, what you need to do in order to grow, reach a level of profitability, and then build on to move into prosperity.

If financial planning is not one of your primary skills, there is absolute value in engaging a professional to do this for you. If you engage a professional, the plan should be to make it a long term relationship so you get to know each other, define what help you need, on what basis and frequency, how the data can be collected then moved into a reporting frequency and cycle. Once all this is in place, the data needs to be thoroughly interpreted and analyzed so it gives you a road map of where your business has come from, where it is now, and where it is going.

Below I've touched on five financial tools made of Excel spreadsheets you may find useful for your business. The type of business you build and the industry will determine the final make up of the financial tools you need.

Each of the tools described below is from an Excel spreadsheet or Word document put together by SCORE. You can download these files from my website at http://www.Andrew-Rogerson.com. Once this page loads, on the left hand side there is a menu of options. Towards the bottom choose the option called 'Sample Documents' and you will see different Word and Excel files. Please select the document you need.

Start Up Expense Planner

As you start planning your new business it will be a good idea to know what your initial out of pocket expenses will be so you can make sure you have cash available to cover those costs. The spreadsheet below gives you an example to follow. Obviously change the columns to suit your business.

Item or Service	Quantity	Budget	Actual Cost	Variation	Date bought
Computer(s)	2	$1,000	$700	$300	
Printer - Color Laser	1	$350	$300	$50	
Monitor	2	$350	$400	-$50	
Software (s)	2	$600	$500	$100	
Desks	2	$500	$550	-$50	
Chairs	2	$200	$150	$50	
Fax machine	1	$200	$150	$50	
Phone	2	$200	$150	$50	
Telephone lines	2	$100	$120	-$20	
Filing cabinet - 4 Door	1	$50	$80	-$30	
				$0	
Website Design	1	$600	$600	$0	
Website hosting - 12 months	1	$100	$80	$20	
				$0	
Business cards		$100	$100	$0	
Flyers		$300	$300	$0	
				$0	
Business License		$50	$100	-$50	
Legal fees - to create entity		$500	$1,000	-$500	
Accounting advice		$1,000	$1,200	-$200	
				$0	
Marketing consultant		$500	$400	$100	
Insurance - Business		$400	$350	$50	
Insurance - Auto		$500	$600	-$100	
Total costs		$7,600	$7,830	-$230	

If you would like a template created in Excel to use for your business to track your start up expenses, please go to: http://www.Andrew-Rogerson.com. Once this page loads, on the left hand side there is a menu of options. Towards the bottom choose 'Sample Documents'. After this page displays, look for document # 9. Simply download, complete, save, and monitor it to make sure you are staying within your budget. This tool has been created by SCORE.

Sales Forecast – Year One Planner

The purpose of the Sales forecast tool is to project your expected level of sales once your business opens for customers. The spreadsheet below gives you a sample to follow. A sales forecast is an important financial tool as it forms the basis of other decisions such as budgeting and cash flow forecasts. The more accurately you can forecast your sales, the better informed you will be for the other financial tools you use and create.

Fiscal Year Begins	Jan - 08												
12-month Sales Forecast													
	Jan-08	Feb-08	Mar-08	Apr-08	May-08	Jun-08	Jul-08	Aug-08	Sep-08	Oct-08	Nov-08	Dec-08	Annual Totals
Cat 1 units sold	50	55	60	80	120	200	400	280	300	330	400	450	2725
Sale price @ unit	100	100	100	100	105	105	110	110	110	110	110	110	
Cat 1 TOTAL	5,000	5,500	6,000	8,000	12,600	21,000	44,000	30,800	33,000	36,300	44,000	49,500	295,700
Cat 2 units sold	100	100	110	130	130	150	180	120	120	120	135	140	1535
Sale price @ unit	100	100	100	100	100	100	100	100	100	100	100	100	
Cat 2 TOTAL	10,000	10,000	11,000	13,000	13,000	15,000	18,000	12,000	12,000	12,000	13,500	14,000	153,500
Cat 3 units sold	40	40	40	40	45	45	60	30	30	35	40	40	485
Sale price @ unit	50	50	50	50	50	50	50	50	50	50	50	50	
Cat 3 TOTAL	2,000	2,000	2,000	2,000	2,250	2,250	3,000	1,500	1,500	1,750	2,000	2,000	24,250
Cat 4 units sold	20	20	20	25	25	25	30	25	25	25	25	25	290
Sale price @ unit	50	50	50	50	50	50	50	50	50	50	50	50	
Cat 4 TOTAL	1,000	1,000	1,000	1,250	1,250	1,250	1,500	1,250	1,250	1,250	1,250	1,250	14,500
Monthly totals: All Categories	18,000	18,500	20,000	24,250	29,100	39,500	66,500	45,550	47,750	51,300	60,750	66,750	487950

If you would like a template created in Excel to use for your Sales Forecasting, please go to: http://www.Andrew-Rogerson.com. Once this page loads, on the left hand side there is a menu of options. Towards the bottom choose 'Sample Documents'. After this page displays look for document #10. Simply download and save the spreadsheet to your computer and use it as necessary. This tool has been created by SCORE.

Personal Budget Planner

As you begin your journey to start your new business, you may like to review your current personal spending to see if you can make any cutbacks. If you are currently single and have no other responsibilities, it makes sense to see where your current expenditures go and if you can make any cutbacks in the short-term. Conversely, if your family currently has two incomes and will drop to one when you start your business, you may want to do the same by seeing what you can cut back, so you can fund your new business until it becomes profitable.

To help you do that, review the spreadsheet shown below or if you prefer, create your own in Excel and do some "what-if" scenarios. The choices are all yours, however, I would suggest that starting a new business generally costs more and takes longer than most business owners starting out expect, so discretion is the better part of valor.

	A	B	C
1	**Main Item**	**Current Amount**	**Revised amount**
2	Allowances - kids		
3	Auto - Insurance		
4	Auto - gas		
5	Cash		
6	Charitable contributions		
7	Childcare		
8	Clothes		
9	Education		
10	Entertainment		
11	Gifts		
12	Groceries		
13	Hair care		
14	Household costs		
15	Insurance - House & contents		
16	Insurance - Medical		
17	Medical and dental expenses		
18	Miscellaneous		
19	Pet		
20	Property taxes		
21	Rent/Mortgage		
22	Repairs and maintenance		
23	Taxes		
24	Travel		
25	Utilities - Cable		
26	Utilities - Cell		
27	Utilities - Electricity		
28	Utilities - Gas		
29	Utilities - Internet		
30	Utilities - Phone		
31			
32	Total Per Month		
33	Variation		

There is no specific spreadsheet on my website for this but just copy the layout above into Excel and thereby create your own.

Profit And Loss Projection

A Profit and Loss Projection is a planning tool to track your projected sales against your costs to run your business and therefore show how profitable you will be. Below is a very basic P&L projection for 6 months using the sales numbers above from the One Year Sales forecast spreadsheet.

	Jan-08	% B/A	Feb-08	%	Mar-08	%	Apr-08	%	May-08	%	Jun-08	%
Revenue (Sales)												
Category 1	5,000	27.8	5,500	29.7	6,000	30.0	8,000	33.0	12,600	43.3	21,000	53.2
Category 2	10,000	55.6	10,000	54.1	11,000	55.0	13,000	53.6	13,000	44.7	15,000	38.0
Category 3	2,000	11.1	2,000	10.8	2,000	10.0	2,000	8.2	2,250	7.7	2,250	5.7
Category 4	1,000	5.6	1,000	5.4	1,000	5.0	1,250	5.2	1,250	4.3	1,250	3.2
Total Revenue (Sales)	18,000	100.0	18,500	100.0	20,000	100.0	24,250	100.0	29,100	100.0	39,500	100.0
Cost of Sales												
Category 1	2,500	50.0	2,750	50.0	3,000	50.0	4,000	50.0	6,300	50.0	10,000	47.6
Category 2	3,000	30.0	3,000	30.0	3,200	29.1	3,600	27.7	3,600	27.7	4,000	26.7
Category 3	1,000	50.0	1,000	50.0	1,000	50.0	1,000	50.0	1,100	48.9	1,100	48.9
Category 4	100	10.0	100	10.0	100	10.0	120	9.6	120	9.6	120	9.6
Total Cost of Sales	6,600	36.7	6,850	37.0	7,300	36.5	8,720	36.0	11,120	38.2	15,220	38.5
Gross Profit	11,400	63.3	11,650	63.0	12,700	63.5	15,530	64.0	17,980	61.8	24,280	61.5
Expenses												
Salary expenses	2,000	11.1	2,000	10.8	2,000	10.0	2,000	8.2	2,000	6.9	2,000	5.1
Payroll expenses	1,500	8.3	1,500	8.1	1,500	7.5	1,500	6.2	1,500	5.2	1,500	3.8
Outside services	300	1.7	300	1.6	300	1.5	300	1.2	300	1.0	300	0.8
Office supplies	100	0.6	100	0.5	100	0.5	100	0.4	100	0.3	100	0.3
Repairs and maintenance	50	0.3	50	0.3	50	0.3	50	0.2	50	0.2	50	0.1
Advertising	120	0.7	120	0.6	120	0.6	120	0.5	120	0.4	120	0.3
Car, delivery and travel	80	0.4	80	0.4	80	0.4	80	0.3	80	0.3	80	0.2
Accounting and legal	500	2.8		0.0		0.0		0.0		0.0	500	1.3
Rent	400	2.2	400	2.2	400	2.0	400	1.6	400	1.4	400	1.0
Telephone	50	0.3	50	0.3	50	0.3	50	0.2	50	0.2	50	0.1
Utilities	45	0.3	45	0.2	45	0.2	45	0.2	45	0.2	45	0.1
Insurance		0.0		0.0	400	2.0		0.0		0.0		0.0
Taxes (real estate, etc.)		0.0		0.0		0.0		0.0	400	1.4		0.0
Interest	250	1.4	250	1.4	250	1.3	250	1.0	250	0.9	250	0.6
Depreciation	300	1.7	300	1.6	300	1.5	300	1.2	300	1.0	300	0.8
Total Expenses	5,695	31.6	5,195	28.1	5,595	28.0	5,195	21.4	5,595	19.2	5,695	14.4
Net Profit	5,705	31.7	6,455	34.9	7,105	35.5	10,335	42.6	12,385	42.6	18,585	47.1

If you would like your own working document so you can do your own projections, please go to: http://www.Andrew-Rogerson.com. On the left hand side there is a menu of options. Towards the bottom choose 'Sample Documents'. After this page displays look for documents #11 & #12. Download the spreadsheet to your computer and use it. This tool has been created by SCORE.

Other Finance Planning Tools

In addition to the Startup expense spreadsheet, the Sales forecast spreadsheet, and the Personal Budget spreadsheet, a good thing to do before starting your business is to create a Profit and Loss projection for the first year and the first three years. You can also create a cash flow projection so you can understand when you will have to make the actual payments to keep your business open and in good graces with your suppliers, lender and employees. Good business practices may also include doing a competitive analysis and/or breakeven analysis. If you would like to do these there are spreadsheets available. Finally, if you want to create an initial balance sheet and ongoing balance sheet these documents are also available.

All these documents give you reference points as your business builds, and a financial road map to know you are heading in the right direction or make some adjustments to get to your destination.

Cash flow projection

If you would like a working document, please go to: http://www.Andrew-Rogerson.com. When this page loads, on the left hand side there is a menu of options. Towards the bottom choose the option called 'Sample Documents'. After this page displays look for document # 13 & #14.

Breakeven Analysis

If you would like a working document, please go to: http://www.Andrew-Rogerson.com. When this page loads, on the left hand side there is a menu of options. Towards the bottom choose the option called 'Sample Documents'. After this page displays look for document # 15.

Competitive Analysis

If you would like a working document, please go to: http://www.Andrew-Rogerson.com. When this page loads, on the left hand side there is a menu of options. Towards the bottom choose the option called 'Sample Documents'. After this page displays look for document # 16.

Balance Sheets

If you would like a working document, please go to: http://www.Andrew-Rogerson.com. When this page loads, on the left hand side there is a menu of options. Towards the bottom choose the option called 'Sample Documents'. After this page displays look for document # 17 & #18.

Financial Projection Models

If you would like a working document, please go to: http://www.Andrew-Rogerson.com. When this page loads, on the left hand side there is a menu of options. Towards the bottom choose the option called 'Sample Documents'. After this page displays look for document # 19 & #20.

If this is all new to you, SCORE provides a great source of information and help. To find a local SCORE chapter go to their website http://www.score.org and search based on your zip code.

Risk Management

In the previous topic we went through budgets and other finance planning tools. Right behind this subject is risk management. Risk management is basically putting a strategy in place that has the primary focus of looking at the operation of a business to try and determine if all the components of the business are operating correctly and in sync with each other. For example, as you start your business you build with growth in sales, happy customers, and employees which flow to the bottom line. When this happens, this is the time when the owner of the business takes his eye off the ball. Overseas trips, golf once a week with his new found business friends, adding the new and latest sports car to the business or running up large bills for no other reason than the business can afford it.

Risk management can mean different things to different people. It's not the goal of this topic in this guide other than to mention it so you are aware it exists and when the time is right in your business to pay attention to it. Create data points, measure the critical performance levels in the business, and manage them; closely.

Risk management can be applied in the early stages of your business to ensure the budgets and limited capital you have to spend are done within tolerance levels. When they move out of tolerance, it's time to address what's happening and bring it in line with what's been planned. For example, it may be agreed that sales and marketing expenditure is $400 per month until gross sales meet a certain level. The risk management aspect would be to monitor that agreement and if sales are not at the correct level but sales and marketing needs $400 per month (or more) then a cut needs to be made in another area.

Another application of risk management is benchmarking industry standards and seeing how your business is performing against those standards. For example, through research you have found that the Cost of Goods for the type of business you operate in your industry is 40% of gross sales. When you look at your business and find your Cost of Goods is 55% of gross sales, you need to do some work to negotiate lower prices as your competitors are doing better than you. And so it goes on.

You may perceive risk management as something a mature business undertakes. But it has different applications for different stages of a business. When you start your business I expect you will not have the time or resources to focus on it. However, if you are getting professional help they should be able to provide this analysis as part of their service at little to no additional cost.

The 5 steps of good risk management are:
1. Risk Identification is deciding the what, how, and when. Data needs to be measured and then made sure all data is collected the same way each time so the results aren't distorted or irrelevant.
2. Risk Analysis involves categorizing risks, deciding the significance of the risk and if it's important enough to spend resources to fix the problem. This is then followed by risk reviews to make sure everyone's on the same page and the problem doesn't reappear.
3. Risk Response Planning is planning on what steps to take if an element gets out of alignment.
4. Risk Plan Implementation is establishing an action plan once an event is out of alignment.
5. Risk Tracking and Monitoring involves watching to see if the implementation is working. If the problem persists then it goes back to number one for further risk identification for analysis and resolution.

This topic may sound too advanced for a start up business but understanding its logic and methodology can truly allow you to build a powerful business in a shorter time and having it ready to sell should a suitable buyer come along.

If this topic is of interest to you and you would like a working document to help you, please go to my website http://www.Andrew-Rogerson.com. On the left hand side of the Home Page there is a menu of options that includes one towards the bottom called Sample Documents. Click on this menu option and once this page displays you will see different Word and Excel files created by SCORE. Documents 11 & 12 may help though you are welcome to use any of the other documents.

Finance Options

With all the items on the checklist to take care of, often a key component of the deal is you securing financing.

Most franchisors have a process in place for securing a loan for the buyer. This is the normal process but as a business broker I do have contacts with national, regional, and local lenders who will finance a franchise purchase to a qualified buyer.

To make an application for a loan, you will normally need:

✓ An application form from the lender you will need to complete.
✓ Proof of an acceptable amount for a payment including proof if it is in cash (* See **Note** below.)
✓ A minimum credit score acceptable to the lender (this varies but is about 680 on the FICO and up.)
✓ Supporting documents for the loan such as tax returns, payroll stubs to show previous wages, and income, business plan plus many other documents as it relates to the transaction.

Finance may also be required for funding working capital or Accounts Receivable or assets of the business such as vehicles or office equipment. In some cases, financing can be provided by the franchisor but in most cases it will be provided by a third party.

To minimize frustration, early in the process disclose to the franchisor you will need finance and that it will be a condition on which to make your purchase. The franchisor can then explain their arrangements so you can do the appropriate research to see if the finance is acceptable to you at the right terms and conditions.

Consider securing funding for the downpayment from different sources such as family, friends, banks or credit unions. These are not necessarily typical sources of funds for every buyer, but other options include:
✓ Home equity loan
✓ Local banks
✓ Small Business Administration (SBA)

If you have money in a 401k plan and would like to use this as downpayment to buy a business, more information is available from companies that specialize in this sort of funding. More information is available in Section 8 called "Other finance options."

* **Note**: As we are talking about money, a franchise buyer will need to have a downpayment available, in cash, to buy almost any franchise. If a downpayment is not readily available it is one of the first

things I would get in place before talking to franchisors otherwise you may waste a lot of time and energy, and create a lot of frustration not only for yourself but also for others.

If this topic is of interest to you and you would like a working document to help you, please go to my website http://www.Andrew-Rogerson.com. On the left hand side of the Home Page there is a menu of options that includes one towards the bottom called Sample Documents. Click on this menu option and once this page displays you will see different Word and Excel files created by SCORE. Documents 4, 5 & 6 may help though you are welcome to use any of the other documents.

Sources of additional information include:

SBA Loan program:	http://www.sba.gov
Small Business finance:	http://www.vfinance.com
Finance options:	http://www.business.com/Finance.asp
CNN Money:	http://money.cnn.com/index.html
Federal Government Small Business Finance:	http://www.business.gov/guides/finance

Site Assessment

If you've decided to rent or lease retail, office or warehouse space, below is a worksheet to help you start this most important task. Add, move or change any of the headings as they apply to your situation but try to be as prepared as you can on what you want so you don't waste time and money searching for what you want. Plus, if you seek professional help, the more organized you are the better they will respond.

Should you hire a professional such as a Commercial Real Estate agent help you find the right space? Absolutely! The only exception to this is if you work as a Commercial Real Estate agent and therefore have the experience to do the negotiations and understand the legal documents to go with leasing or renting property. You can drive around and see the "For lease" signs, jot down phone numbers and call the Commercial Real Estate agents. But they are the agent of the owner of the property and so their legal responsibility is to represent them and their interests. A lease is a complex legal document. Accepting it at face value is not in your best interests, plus negotiating price and terms is something the owner's agent will have done many times and so will have an advantage over you if you try and do it yourself.

Tenant Improvements

An item to negotiate with the owner/agent is tenant improvements. For example, if you plan to open a restaurant and the space you wish to lease is brand new, the owner will almost definitely have made a provision of money to attract a new tenant to cover the costs of creating internal walls, fixtures, flooring such as tiles or carpet, and may be even equipment. Part of your discussion with the owner/agent should include the question, how much money is available for tenant improvements?

Security deposit and insurance

The lease will breakdown the details of the legal contract between you and the owner. Make sure you allow for the first month's rent plus there will be a requirement that you pay with the first month's rent a refundable security deposit that could be anywhere from one to two month's rent. The security deposit is refundable at the end of the lease as long as the property is in good condition. Normal wear and tear is accepted.

Lease duration

An important item in your lease is its duration. As you are just starting out, committing to a long term lease may not be in your interest. What can help or harm your negotiations is the condition of the local economy where you are based. If the local economy is strong then rents will be high with little room for negotiation. If the economy is soft, you'll have more flexibility. Part of your juggling act when deciding what lease duration to sign, is how quickly you think you will grow. The solution is to get a lease that allows you to assign the lease to another party. Make sure this provision is included in the lease. Be careful not to get a condition that allows you to sub-lease the property as this requires you to pay the owner regardless and collect money from the new tenant. If the new tenant doesn't pay you, you still have to pay the owner.

Site assessment worksheet

Use the worksheet below to record your assessment of each location that makes good business sense to you. After you've seen several different properties that are suitable, sit down with all your worksheets to narrow it down to at least three suitable options. When you first inquired you would have been given rates per square foot plus any other costs involved in leasing the property, however, now it's time to really start negotiations with the owner or his agent using your commercial real estate agent that is representing you. Move between the three best options until you have the best deal you can get, sign your lease and move onto the next item in your business plan. If you have questions about the legalese in the lease, consult a qualified attorney as once you've signed the lease you have entered into a binding contract.

Name of Building/Shopping Center:	
Address:	
Cross Street:	
Anchor Store/Nearby Businesses:	
Utilities Included?	
Average Operating Hours of Neighboring Businesses:	
Security?	
Parking Availability, Cost, and Proximity:	
Proximity to Competition:	
Storage Area Size & Description:	
Kitchen Area Detail:	
Bathroom Area Detail:	
Back Office Area Detail:	
General Description of Property:	
Color and Condition of Flooring:	
Any Fixtures Included?	
Repairs/Improvements needed?	
Signage: Can I display my business name above my suite?	
Signage: Is there a display on the street front that displays all the tenants for customers to see?	

Freeway Access?		Public Transit Access?	
Square Footage:		Foot Traffic?	
Price:		NNN/CAM Charges?	
Street Visibility?		Marquee Signage?	
Central Heat?		Central A/C?	
Age of Roof:		Building Last Painted:	

Write any additional questions you would like to research:

Notes:

Professionals You Can Hire

One of your many decisions is what professional help you will need, if any, to start your business. Any help you choose to hire will start with your skill set. If you are a marketing consultant by profession you don't need to hire that skill. If you have family or friends that are attorneys or accountants you've got that one covered.

In the very initial stage of starting your business, my suggestion is to avoid hiring too much professional help. At this stage of your business you are in the fact finding and exploring phase and your needs may change. To have spent money on professional advice to then find it's no longer relevant because you've decided to do something else is not a good return on your investment. Initially gather knowledge, information, and names of good professionals so when the time is right to hire their services, you are clear on the help you need and spend your money wisely.

Attributes

In the next topic we will look at the different type of professionals you can hire. However, here are some thoughts on the type of attributes you may look for in that professional.

Accreditation

If you are looking for a professional with a specific skill set, then their accreditation will tell you the education they have obtained for that specialized skill. There are literally hundreds of three and four letter accreditations. To see if that accreditation is what you are looking for, simply do a Google search. Another option is to find their website and read about their education levels to make sure their academic expertise is what you want.

Compensation

Is the advisor being compensated by commissions on the sale or are they charging you a fee for a service? Some advisors have a combination where they get a fee for a certain part of their time but also can get commission if they make a sale. Fully understand how they are compensated to make sure it makes sense to you.

Business knowledge and experience

Going to college, reading and passing the courses, and networking with small business owners is nice. However, where the rubber hits the road, it is experience that counts. Look for someone who understands the dynamics, pressures, stresses and responsibilities that business ownership demands. This should be one of the foremost skills you need from any small business advisor. The best way of finding that person probably comes from networking with other small business owners who have "been there and done that."

Expert network

A good advisor should have a strong network of accountants, attorneys, consultants, lenders and other specialists they can refer to you. Referrals are the main stay of most advisors because the work they do often permeates into other disciplines. Their work is therefore exposed to other professionals that get to know not only the advisor's professional work, but also their reputation.

Goal and style synergy

You may meet many advisors but what you are looking for is *the right one*. If honesty and trust are important to you, that will be the type of advisor that will work best for you. Similarly, as you work with an advisor you will build a relationship, and so it is important the person you are dealing with understands what you are about and is able to communicate clearly. As mentioned earlier, if the advisor just wants to use buzzwords and jargon to inflate their importance, then that may not be the type of advisor you want working with you.

Reputation and references

As a business owner you value word of mouth and your reputation. It is therefore rewarding to thank professionals you think highly of by using their services again, or referring them to somebody you know that needs that same service. However, a lot of the work the advisors do is highly confidential so they have to be careful when handing out references. If a referral is given unsolicited from a "happy customer" that you know professionally, that should give you encouragement to further inquire about using that professional's services.

Services you can hire

A lot of business owners are reluctant to hire professionals. Reasons include their belief that the cost is too high, the professional doesn't know as much about their business choices as they do, the business owner cannot readily find the right person, or someone they know used that service and had a bad experience.

If the right professional is hired for the right reason, the value they bring should far outweigh their cost. This value will be in saving you time, not only in terms of hours spent, but giving back your time so you can spend it on more profitable areas. The two primary important reasons though to hire a professional are because of the expertise they bring to solve a problem or providing an impartial perspective to an unexpected situation. The tax, finance, accounting, legal, human resources, and business laws are complex. The right professional can quickly navigate you through these areas.

Here are some thoughts on each of the different types of professionals you may need to hire, how to find them, and most importantly, knowing if they are the right fit for you. I've also included blank templates so you can write down questions that come to mind that you may want to ask each of these professionals.

Accountant/Tax Advisor

There are three types of accounting professionals a business owner may consider hiring to assist with the sale of the business. These are a Certified Public Accountant (CPA), tax attorney or a personal financial planner. The option chosen will likely come down to cost and the specifics you need to address.

The above list is not to suggest that others can't assist. For example, there are many street-wise and highly skilled bookkeepers that may have intimate knowledge of a business and can readily advise you. However, if you are looking for a professional to hire and you have no existing relationships, then these are the professionals to consider.

Resources for Locating CPAs:
American Institute of Certified Public Accountants	http://www.aicpa.org
Thomas Financial	http://www.thomasonfinancial.com

Tax Attorneys:
Lawyers.com	http://www.lawyers.com
National Association of Enrolled Agents	http://www.naea.org/MemberPortal
Findlaw.com	http://www.findlaw.com

Sources of additional information include:
National Association of Financial and Estate Planners	http://www.nafep.com/index.html
Risk Management Association	http://www.rmahq.org/RMA
Walker Advisory Associates	http://www.waa-online.com/new/waaonline

Accounting/Tax Questions you want to research or ask.

If you have any accounting or tax questions you have been thinking about or they come to mind as you read this guide, write them down here so you can research then at the appropriate time.

Attorney

Just as there are specialists in finance and accounting due to the breadth of the subject, so too are there experts in the different fields of law. It is important that you find an attorney who specializes in the specific area of law you need, in this case, business law. Your attorney will not only be able to guide you through the legalese of starting your business but with any help creating your legal entity such as a corporation, company or partnership.

Resources for Locating Attorneys:

The American Bar Association:	http://www.abanet.org
Your state's Bar Association:	http://www.abanet.org/barserv/stlobar.html
	http://www.lawyers.com

Sources of additional information include:

http://www.abanet.org/public.html
http://www.legalzoom.com
http://www.nolo.com
http://www.lesi.org
http://www.bizfilings.com
http://public.findlaw.com

Legal Questions to Research

If you have any legal questions you have been thinking about or they come to mind as you read this guide, write them down here so you can research then at the appropriate time.

Business Broker or Business Intermediary

Business brokers, also known as Business Intermediaries, provide a range of services to help buyers and sellers enter and exit business ownership respectively. The best reason to use a business broker is that they have an in-depth knowledge of the buying and selling process and the necessary license which some States require. This advantage can be tremendous as you can engage the services of a business broker to help you find a business for sale or a franchise or both. As you work through your business ownership options, it's good to work with the one consultant so they get to know what is and isn't working for you, but most importantly, develop a level of trust so you know your interests are being looked after. If you don't think this is happening, regardless of who you are working with, look for a new broker. Your broker plays a critical role in being a sounding board for you as well as understanding all the processes, forms and relationships you may need.

The International Business Brokers Association (IBBA) is a global organization and has the largest membership of business brokers in the United States. It provides a forum for the industry including education standards for business brokers to obtain accreditation with the designation of Certification of Business Intermediary (CBI).

Sources of additional information include:

International Business Brokers Association   http://www.ibba.org
Murphy Business and Financial   http://www.murphybusiness.com

Business Broker/Consultant questions to research

If you have any questions regarding personal financial planning you have been thinking about or they come to mind as you read this guide, write them down here so you can research then at the appropriate time.

Marketing consultant

A great professional service to consider when starting your business is the services of a marketing consultant. There are business consultants and business coaches available, but their expertise is more geared to help you at a personal level to stay motivated, provide a sounding board, keep you focused, etc. The role of a marketing consultant is to help you build your Business Plan and then help or provide the research for you on your best target market, how to brand yourself, create a business name and then build a sales and marketing plan. A good marketing consultant will also have great networking relationships and be able to suggest good people you could connect with to grow your business.

Marketing consultants generally charge an hourly rate for their time like an accountant or attorney. My business is based in Sacramento and I have found an excellent Marketing Coach called Mon Hart. If you are interested in knowing the services she provides as a Marketing Coach visit her website at http://www.themarketingcoach.us. You can see the services she provides and then search the web to see if you have a local person in your market who can assist you. She also has an interesting link on her website that suggests what to look for if you plan to hire a marketing consultant. The current web link is as follows but bear in mind this may change.
http://www.themarketingcoach.us/selectcoach.html

Marketing Consultant questions to research

If you have any questions regarding personal financial planning you have been thinking about or they come to mind as you read this guide, write them down here so you can research then at the appropriate time.

Personal Financial Planner

Earlier in this section we discussed whether hiring an accountant or tax advisor was necessary. We mentioned that a personal financial planner may be an option that works for some sellers, especially if the planner you are considering hiring is experienced in advising on financial statements. Specific skills or characteristics to consider when looking for a personal financial planner include the following:

Accreditation

There are literally dozens of three and four letter accreditations. These include specializations such as CLU (Chartered Life Underwriter) for life insurance or QPA (Qualified Pension Administrator) for business retirement and benefit plans. Investment advisors must register with the Securities and Exchange Commission and become RIAs (Registered Investment Advisors). Advisors with more sophisticated training include Certified Financial Planners (CFP) and ChFC (Chartered Financial Consultant).

Compensation

When hiring a financial planner, there are three compensation options available. First, they can be compensated by commissions on the sales of investment and insurance products. Second, they can be fee-based only, or third, they can charge you a fee for a service but also can get commissions for products they sell.

Sources of additional information include:

Certified Financial Planner Board of Standards	http://www.cfp.net
Chartered Financial Consultant	http://www.chfc-clu.com

Personal Financial Planner questions to research

If you have any questions regarding personal financial planning you have been thinking about or they come to mind as you read this guide, write them down here so you can research then at the appropriate time.

Virtual Assistant

A great new service has gained traction recently from a highly skilled group of people that for different reasons have decided they do not want to be part of the formal employment community by working for a company or corporation but obviously need a source of income to buy their food, pay the mortgage and have vacations like everyone else. They may be stay-at-home Moms or people who prefer only to work part-time. For business owners with limited resources they are a great option as you can delegate a task to them with a deadline and wait for the finished work to come back to you. No on-the-job training, no payroll taxes, no sick leave or unplanned absence – they take care of all this themselves. You get to define your problem, compare the solution you see with them, and let them take care of the rest.

I've personally started using Virtual Assistants in my work and have seen others use them. I definitely see the upside. Like all things though you need to be careful. Their hourly rate may be much higher than an employee and this is because their time is project-based and temporary. They are running their own business so need to cover their costs to get the work done not knowing if a 10 hour assignment is really 10 hours or 15. Plus because they are timeline driven they have to meet that deadline or run the risk of not being paid or losing a customer they have taken time to build a relationship with.

The downsides are having the person available when you need them. Also, if a job is too complex and the Virtual Assistant has no history behind the project, they may do a bunch of work to find out it's not what you want.

However, for somebody starting a business that needs a Business Plan, Sales and Marketing Plan, advertisement, series of spreadsheets, a sales flyer or similar one off project, a Virtual Assistant can be a great option – especially if you find one that understands what you do and doesn't need extensive training.

Virtual Assistant questions to research

If you have any questions regarding a virtual assistant you have been thinking about or they come to mind as you read this guide, write them down here so you can research then at the appropriate time.

Jargon And Buzzwords

There are different professionals you may engage or will be forced to do business with whether you like it or not. Some of them have a direct influence such as an attorney, accountant, landlord, banker, tax agent, personal financial planner or business coach, while others have an indirect role.

Each group of professionals tends to have its own business jargon and methodologies. If these terms seem confusing, stop and ask for a clear explanation. Don't let the jargon used exclude you from understanding what's happening – there is no such thing as a stupid question. This is your life and business – make sure it ALL makes complete sense to you. This is your responsibility. As I mentioned earlier, don't forget the glossary of terms at the back of this guide as it may assist you.

Write down industry jargon or buzzwords you want to research and better understand.

End Of Chapter Notes

Use this page to write down notes, ideas and other brainstorming for starting your business.

Research
&
Planning

"Being busy does not always mean real work. The object of all work is production or accomplishment and to either of these ends there must be forethought, system, planning, intelligence, and honest purpose, as well as perspiration. Seeming to do is not doing."

Thomas A. Edison

Introduction

Sections One and Two cover a lot of the basic terms and concepts when starting your own business. The focus of Section Three is three-fold. First, it is to do some research about the business idea you have to determine if there is a market for your business, or more importantly, a market that will allow you to not only cover your costs but also make money. Second, develop a plan using different documents and strategies so you can start your business, hit the ground running, and build momentum to your ultimate success. Third, bring all you've learnt together so you have purpose, focus, and success so if you receive interest from a buyer to purchase your business, you can make that ultimate decision with as much knowledge as possible.

Just a Reminder

This is a workbook. It is meant for writing, scribbling and making notes. Staple into the pages any notes you take or articles you read. It requires you making notes, finding, reading and writing questions, along with reminders and inspirations about documents or processes. By the time you finish this section you will have available the information a buyer or professional you hire may need. The remaining sections of this book then capture the flow of the transaction and the best practices to follow. Now, let's do some research!

Research: The Foundation For Success

Before you leap into the everyday running of your business, the more information you have about your customers, means the more successful you will be. Once you move into accepting business your energy and focus will need to be delivering as high a standard as possible so your customer word of mouth is positive, and your business sales increase. There are a number of ways to research your market. Briefly these include:
1. Hiring a marketing consultant to work with you to build the research and then do the research for you.
2. Create and conduct your own research.
3. A combination of the above two where you have a marketing consultant put the initial ideas together with you, and then you hire people to do the research for you, such as marketing college students.

If you are starting a business and money is tight, option two is probably the one you are going to use. So let's quickly understand market research

Market research involves testing the market to determine the acceptance of a particular product or service, especially amongst different demographics. It is used to establish which segment of your market will or does purchase a product or service using a baseline of variables such as age, gender, location, income level, and many other variables you've identified. Quality market research allows companies to learn more about past, current, and potential customers, including their specific likes and dislikes to arrive at a specific data point called a target market or target audience. A target audience is a specific group of customers that has a distinct need or desire for a product or service. Once a target market has been identified, a marketing message can be created and then modified based on further feedback thereby creating a constantly improving dynamic. Further market research can then be used to determine how often the target audience will buy a particular item, how much they are willing to pay, and their overall satisfaction with it.

Define And Understand Your Market

With the above in mind, a critical piece of information any business owner needs to know is their target market. To use an extreme example, everyone needs to drink water. We can get it for free from a faucet, or pay for it from a machine outside a grocery store, or buy it in a plastic bottle with all sorts of brand names on it at convenience stores, gas stations etc to name a few. If you've decided to sell water you have to know which customers will pay for it, how much they will they pay, how often, and how do they want to buy it. It's critical to understand the market need for your product or service otherwise you could invest too much time and money to find out the customer won't pay the price you need to be profitable. Remember, it's much easier to fill a need than to create one. So let's do some research and get some answers to the following questions:

Is the market saturated with businesses like yours? Or is there room in the marketplace for your business?

If no businesses like yours exist in the marketplace, why not?

Does your business fit a consumer need? What is it? Why will customers need your product/service?

How will your business be better than the competition? Will you compete on price, quality, or service?

Who are your target customers (age, income level, interests, etc.)? Where are they located?

Market Research

I think you'll agree it makes perfect sense to determine if your business is viable and if you will be able to make a living. The starting place to do this is a demographics analysis so you understand and can then build your target market or audience. Demographics is simply the art of getting information about individuals or groups such as age, gender, income, marital status, home ownership, presence of children, etc. Once you've identified your target audience, get out there and talk to them. Once you know the composition of your target market you can customize your brand, business name and logo etc. A target audience is a specific group of customers that has a distinct need or desire for a product or service.

Once you have your target market you can obtain further information online. This is a great website for getting general demographic information - http://www.melissadata.com

You can also purchase industry reports from sources like www.firstresearch.com or www.ibisworld.com

---

Identify questions that will help you better understand your market:

Interview your target customers to gain a better understanding of the demand for your products/services.

Have you ever used a product or service like this before?

What are the three things you like the most and three things you dislike the most?

What are the benefits you see with a product/service like this?

How much would *you* be willing to pay for a product/service like this?

What features do you think are the most attractive for a product/service like this?

Interview your target customers to gain a better understanding of the demand for your products/services.

Have you ever used a product or service like this before?

What are the three things you like the most and three things you dislike the most?

What are the benefits you see with a product/service like this?

How much would *you* be willing to pay for a product/service like this?

What features do you think are the most attractive for a product/service like this?

Price And Your Competition

For some products or service, the only differentiating factor is price. Even if price is not as critical as that, it's wise to do proper research on your product or service so you have a bench mark and starting point. Create a list of your top ten products or services then find out what each of your competitors charges for the same product/service. Use the findings to determine how you will price your offerings bearing in mind every product you sell doesn't need to be the cheapest. If price is your sole strategy then give careful thought to a single strategy.

Competitor Name:

Product/Service Description	Competitor's Price

Competitor Name:

Product/Service Description	Competitor's Price

Competitor Name:

Product/Service Description	Competitor's Price

Competitor Name:

Product/Service Description	Competitor's Price

Outsell Your Competition With Your USP

The next analysis is to look at the sales and marketing used by your competitors so you can understand what they are doing to make themselves appear in the market as unique. Once you understand what your competition is doing, it will then be time to make your USP. What's a USP? A USP is Unique Selling Position. Most customers buy from a business because that business provides at least one advantage that is important to that customer compared to a competitor. A USP could be location, vast range of products, wonderful and superior customer service, lowest price, most knowledgeable employees, friendliest atmosphere, best refunds policy, highest quality, and so the list goes on. It is almost impossible to be all things to all people and it's virtually impossible to do in business. The highest quality at the lowest price will appeal to some customer segments but so will the highest quality and the highest price.

Pick up some brochures from your competitors and visit their websites to analyze their sales copy. Look to find the USP's they use in their sales pitch. Once you identify those points, define your response. Good salespeople need to fully understand the competition in order to out-sell them. Your responses can later be used during sales calls or in helping to develop your own brochure and website copy that focus on your USP.

Here are some components or combination of components to consider as you build your USP. They will vary depending on your industry:
- ✓ Quality
- ✓ Selection
- ✓ Fashion/styling
- ✓ Price
- ✓ Service
- ✓ Location
- ✓ Product or service guarantee/warranty
- ✓ Exchange policy
- ✓ Refund policy
- ✓ Quality of employees

As you collect information about your competitors, look at their different modes. One may be a strength you can only match but not compete directly against while you may have an advantage you can exploit. For example, your competitor may have the best location in town but when you phone for customer service they are rude, or don't answer the call promptly, or direct you somewhere else for a particular service. Similarly, they may not respond to emails or voicemails, or their price guarantee or refunds policy is inferior, their range of products or services is limited and so you can exploit these situations. Also, because they are in a high profile location their rent is probably very high so your strategy may be a lower rent location with much more aggressive pricing.

It's looking at these details that can reveal competitive opportunities that can enable a business starting out gain traction in the market and become successful.

The templates below provide a tool for you to collect and record data so you can analyze to determine the strengths and weaknesses of your competitors and what you can take from that to build your USP. Add your own ideas as they apply to the industry and business you are considering so you start your new business from a position of strength.

Competitor Name:
Address:

Competitor's Unique Selling Position:

Your strategy:

Competitor's Unique Selling Position:

Your strategy:

Competitor's Unique Selling Position:

Your strategy:

Competitor's Unique Selling Position:

Your strategy:

Competitor Name:
Address:

Competitor's Unique Selling Position:

Your strategy:

Competitor's Unique Selling Position:

Your strategy:

Competitor's Unique Selling Position:

Your strategy:

Competitor's Unique Selling Position:

Your strategy:

Competitor Name:
Address:

Competitor's Unique Selling Position:

Your strategy:

Competitor's Unique Selling Position:

Your strategy:

Competitor's Unique Selling Position:

Your strategy:

Competitor's Unique Selling Position:

Your strategy:

Interview Business Owners

Information is a tool for success. The more you know the better prepared and quicker you are able to react. A great source of information is therefore an entrepreneur who is already doing what you plan to do. They have real world experience and depending on their generosity to share it, can help you avoid making many mistakes. If you are able to secure the time of an entrepreneur who is willing to share, cherish the opportunity, and prepare so you don't waste time. The depth of your questions will also reflect on you and the willingness of the entrepreneur to share with you. The higher the quality of the questions, the more time they will give, as they would welcome questions from somebody with a similar interest as theirs. A suggestion is to offer to buy them coffee or lunch in exchange for some time to spend with them. Perhaps you are thinking – should I interview somebody that is not a competitor? And the answer is yes! The best way to find people who will talk to you is through a Trade Association. Find a trade association that closely matches your business and call them to ask for names of people who you could call.

Here are some interview questions, make sure you add your own:

> **How did you start your business and how many employees did you have?**

> **What were the three biggest challenges you faced when launching your business?**

> **What are the three biggest challenges running your business today?**

> **What would you do differently if you started over today?**

> **What marketing strategies have and haven't worked for you?**

> **How long did it take you to transition from a startup to a successful business and how long did this take?**

What have you learned along the way?

What do you think are the keys to your success?

What advice do you have for me?

How did you finance the start of your business?

Additional questions you'd like to ask:

Here are some interview questions; make sure you add your own:

> How did you start your business and how many employees did you have?

> What were the three biggest challenges you faced when launching your business?

> What are the three biggest challenges running your business today?

> What would you do differently if you started over today?

> What marketing strategies have and haven't worked for you?

> How long did it take you to transition from a startup to a successful business and how long did this take?

> What have you learned along the way?

> What do you think are the keys to your success?

> What advice do you have for me?

How did you finance the start of your business?

Additional questions you'd like to ask:

Life Plan

As you will find when you read the following sections, I am big on planning. There are a number of important reasons for this, and these are:

1. By definition, making a plan requires thinking. When you are into a project, thinking strategically is often not possible as there is so much happening "now" that you put off the planning piece until you get around to it. Too often you find that when you do get around to it, time, money, energy, direction, and opportunities have been lost.
2. After you go through the work of creating a plan, share it and communicate it so those affected and responsible for the plan feel included, know where they fit in, the direction everyone is going, and so they are energized. If you don't have a plan then the exact opposite happens to what I've described and key employees decide to leave as this is not the place they want to continue to work.
3. Once you have created a plan, it gives you a useable format to measure benchmarks and performance. If these are not being met, then the plan can be revisited and changed. And the good news is that you don't have to start all over again but can tweak what's been done, saving so much time, frustration, and missed opportunities.

Business Plan

This is one of the smallest topics in this guide but probably the most important. In my opinion, one of the most important things a business owner needs to do is write a business plan and create a budget and review both documents periodically. The business plan becomes the road map for the new business owner as it forces questions which therefore create or force answers. And it's through both the questions and answers you will be able to determine the best direction for your new business.

Not everyone will agree this is the way to go, but it's easy to see if this makes sense by looking at the questions below. All these questions should be typical to most business plans. And that's one of the points. Each business will have things that are unique to its business so a good plan has to be flexible. You can start with a core document and then simply add or remove items as they apply to your business and make sense to you. And remember, one of the best things about a business plan is that it records where you are at, at a certain moment. A business plan is a living and breathing document and needs to be revisited and updated so it stay fresh but keeps you focused and accountable on what needs to be done in the short term and what can and should be moved into the long term.

Within a good business plan is a good budget that also keeps you focused and accountable. If the business is doing better than expected you can ramp up the growth strategy you devised for the business. If the business is not growing as fast as anticipated, you can see the weaknesses and implement solutions to turn things around.

Most business plans have complementary documents attached to it. For example, a good business plan also needs a good Sales and Marketing plan and finance document, which we talk about a little further in this topic. Plus, I suggest you have an additional document called a Productivity Plan. The Business Plan defines the strategic direction of the business, the Sales and Marketing Plan how it sells your product or service, and the Productivity Plan provides a tactical breakdown of steps to take so it all comes together with the success of the business.

Which Business Plan do I use?

There are many software programs available that have different Business Plan templates. Simply search the web and choose the one that works for you. The best news is that they are free. There are a couple of alternatives. First, go to my website http://www.Andrew-Rogerson.com. Once this page loads, on the left hand side there is a menu of options. Towards the bottom there is one called 'Sample Documents.' Click on this option and once this page displays you will see different Word and Excel files. Document #7 is a Business Plan for a start up business while document #8 is a Business Plan for an established business. Both files are documents created by SCORE. There are also other documents on my website that you are welcome to download and use.

The second alternative is to discuss this with your business broker or consultant and see what they use. They may have an option to share with you and if you follow this option and have questions about how to get it completed, they could readily assist you with that.

The third alternative is to create your own from the suggestion below. A complete business plan can range from 10-100 pages. Your plan should be a work in progress so be sure to write it using a word processing system so you can make changes and update it over time.

Sample Business Plan

I. Company Description/Overview

    A. Nature of Business

        1. Individuals being served/their needs
        2. Why your area?

    B. Your Distinctive Competencies (primary factors that will lead to your success)

        1. Superior customer need satisfaction
        2. Production/service delivery efficiencies
        3. Personnel
        4. Geographic location

II. Market Analysis

    A. Target Markets

        1. Demographics
        2. Geographic location
        3. Seasonal/cyclical trends

    B. Competition

        1. Identification
        2. Strengths (competitive advantages)
        3. Weaknesses (competitive disadvantages)

III. Products and Services

    A. Detailed Product/Service Description (from the user's perspective)

        1. Specific benefits of product/service
        2. Ability to meet needs
        3. Competitive advantages

IV. Marketing and Sales Activities

    A. Overall Market Strategy

        1. Market penetration strategy
            a. Intended means (including advertising, promotion, printed matter, etc.).
        2. Growth Strategy

V. Management and Ownership

    A. Management Staff Structure

    B. Key Managers (including self)

        1. Name
        2. Position
        3. Primary responsibilities and authority
        4. Primary responsibilities and authority with previous employers
        5. Unique skills and experiences that add to your company's distinctive competencies

    C. Legal Structure of the Business

VI. Organization and Personnel

    A. Recruitment procedures

    B. Staffing Levels

8 Important Functions Of A Business Plan

Most small business owners and future entrepreneurs have probably read and heard how it is important to have a business plan. As I travel through my world as a business broker I am surprised to see that very few business owners actually have one, or if they have it, rarely look at it and pay attention to it. If finance is required to grow the business, the business owner puts together a business plan, secures the finance, and promptly forgets about it. You may not realize, however, the benefits of a business plan expand well beyond that single use. It is also a critical tool for your use as you develop and grow your business and here's why.

The business plan is a written document that clearly identifies and defines the goals of a business and precisely outlines the methods for achieving them. It provides a complete and detailed description of how the business will operate and just as importantly, a communications tool not only for investors but also the key management of the business, and others interested in understanding the operations and goals of your business. Your business plan is a living and breathing document and a blueprint on how you are going to build your company. Here are 8 important functions of your business plan:

1. A road map for your initial crucial startup decisions.

It is a management and financial "road map." In short, it is your most important guide to starting, building, and managing a successful business.

2. The place to clarify your ideas and plan of action.

It explains how the business will function in the marketplace. It describes what you are selling, your background and qualifications, who your prospective customers are, where they can be found, what is needed to build the business, how you plan to promote, and determine the viability of the venture in a designated market.

3. It is an operational tool.

The business plan is a tool that clearly depicts characteristics which, when properly used, will help you manage your business and work toward its success. It is a means for communicating your ideas to others by measuring operational progress.

4. A financial tool.

By determining how much money will be needed for start-up costs, it details how the business will be financed. And, as a prospectus for potential investors, it is an important tool to help obtain financing by anticipating ongoing capital and cash requirements to reassure lenders or backers.

5. Place to benchmark and establish best practices.

The finished business plan will be a strategic operational tool that complements the sales and marketing plan and tactical productivity plan to provide guidance to the entrepreneur in organizing planning activities to help move the business forward. A business plan is all about the business, its goals, and its road map to achieving those goals.

6. Future growth.

This is the place to explain how you plan to keep your business growing. It is a detailed guide of what you are going to do and how you are going to increase your profits. These plans should outline your specific goals for the coming one, two and three years. By breaking your objectives down into quarterly, semi-annual and annual milestones, your plan will give you foundations and roots to provide a realistic determinant of your ultimate success. If your Business Plan is still a work in progress or been neglected for more than one quarter, now is the time. Your company's success depends on it!

7. A place to record goals and metrics for accountability.

A business plan is a place to write down short term and long term goals and hold all stakeholders accountable in reaching those goals. If it is written down and you choose to walk away from agreements or milestones, you do so at the peril of the business failing.

8. A place to be honest.

This may sound simplistic, but it's the place to be honest. You can write things down in a business plan and then forget about it. What a waste of time. Or you can embrace the Business Plan and what it stands for, and regularly check you are executing the strategy that everyone bought into and thereby keep not only your team, but also you, focused.

Importance of your Business Plan

If the above section on the importance of a business plan makes sense to you, it will have more meaning as you work with and create your own business plan. A business plan forces discipline and accountability, which what a business is all about. It allows you to be creative and write down what you are thinking so you can come back to it at any time and see if you are going in the direction you planned. If you've wandered off track, the business plan will allow you to see that and re-focus.

In my opinion, the number one reason for creating a business plan is that it works with your sales and marketing plan and productivity plan. The Business plan covers strategic goals and vision, the sales and marketing plan is the what, where, when and how to achieve to achieve the goals of the business. The Productivity plan is a blend of the business and sales and marketing plan by breaking down into tasks and responsibilities with what needs to be done on a daily and weekly basis.

The biggest complaint I hear about a business plan is that you have to keep it up to date. Absolutely – that's its primary purpose. If your business plan is out of date it means you have started in a different direction that you planned. But it means your business plan must be brought up to date so you are forced to consider the direction you are drifting in case that direction is wrong.

Finally, as the owner of the business, you own your Business Plan. If it doesn't work for you it won't work for anybody else. It's as simple as that!

Create And Build Your Sales And Marketing Foundations

Sales and marketing is an extremely broad subject. Large corporations have a sales division and a marketing division. This leads to interesting dynamics where the sales department thinks they are more important than the marketing department while the marketing department knows for a fact it's the other way round. In case you are wondering about the difference, very simply, the marketing department does the analysis and research to find which customers to target for their product, while the sales department talks to the customers the marketing department identifies.

For a business owner starting out there's bad news and good news. The bad news is that you will probably be both departments for quite some time. When your business grows and you can afford it, you will probably add a sales person to your team so they focus on talking to existing and potential customers to grow your business.

Before you can do any marketing and/or sales you need some basics in place. When you first start out you have a couple of options available to you. You can do the best you can and create what you need yourself and tweak it as you go along, or you can invest in some professional help to try and get the basics done so you present a professional appearance and then tweak it with more knowledge of your market or when you have some money to invest in professional help. Here are some thoughts on some basics such as your brand, business name, and logo or trade mark.

Brand

From my perspective, your brand, whatever you choose to make it, is the MOST important component of your business, and it should never be compromised. When you or one of your employees talk with a customer, supplier, lender, landlord or another employee, they are representing your brand. Your brand includes anything that relates to your business such as your logo, your business name, how you answer the phone, how the employees perceive you as the owner of the business, how you conduct yourself, and so it goes on. To illustrate my point, here are some brands. Test your reaction to them and savor each one. Enron, Coca-Cola, Starbucks, HP, Dell, GM, Ford, Toyota, Princess Diana, Queen Elizabeth, the Pope, Donald Trump, Jack Walsh, Julia Roberts, Russell Crowe, George Clooney, Brad Pitt, Barack Obama, United Airlines, Jet Blue, British Airways, Singapore Airlines, and finally Australia.

I understand you will probably argue that Princess Diana, Queen Elizabeth and the Pope etc are not brands but their names are so well known that they have the power to associate themselves with whatever business they are in and as a result, generate business.

Again, from my perspective, we have covered a number of components that I think are linked to your brand. Your vision statement, mission statement, confidentiality policy, privacy policy, refunds policy, clothes you wear (or don't wear), ethics and culture, the way the phone is answered, the quality of the stationery, business cards, advertising material etc that are part of your business. These are all part of your brand.

The bottom line: Let someone or something damage your brand, (which is inexorably linked to your business) and it will affect your bottom line.

10 Steps To A Good Business Name

Your business name is intrinsically linked to your brand and often they are the same. Choosing a good business name requires thought, patience, and perhaps trial and error as you may find the "perfect" business is so perfect somebody else is already using it. Here are 10 things to consider.

1. Mind map or brainstorm ideas. Think out of the box. How do you want customers, employees, vendors, and your family think about your business when they hear its name?

2. If you are in a creative mode and found some business names you like, don't stop. Write down more as the ones you've chosen may not be available. Throw the business names you've thought about around in your head, say them aloud, ask friends, be creative. No suggestion is a bad idea as the bad ideas make you think about the opposite which may be exactly what you are looking for.

3. If you have some ideas you like, use an online dictionary or thesaurus for similar or like meanings. Associate with colors or historical figures or astronomical or astrological associations etc.

4. Talk to people you trust and know you and understand your vision. Your friends will be excited about your new career path and will love to contribute and be part of what you are doing – enjoy the creative process.

5. Prioritize. Throw out any that just don't fit and make a prioritized list of the rest.

6. Once you find some good ideas, make sure they are available by checking for trademarks. Note: It is possible to use a name in a completely different business, but it can create confusion or simply not go together – Coca-Cola Hair Salon or Kraft Auto Repairs?

7. If you find some great names, it's almost mandatory to have a website. Therefore check the domain name is available and if it is, consider registering it before somebody else takes it. I had the unfortunate experience of checking if a domain name was available. It was, but when I went back a week later to register it, somebody had taken it. It's my understanding that some people search the sites you check domain names on, and if you don't register it, they do, so you have to buy it from them.

8. Check Fictitious Business Names or DBA's. If you are a sole proprietor, check with your County Clerk's office to see if the name is available. There's a formal process to follow so get the latest information.

9. Stake your claim! Register your assumed name or file your incorporation papers right away. Also, start using either TM (trademark) or SM (service mark). You do NOT have to register them to use them.

10. If you find the name you want, a U.S. trademark or service mark costs approximately $325. When you are starting out that may be a lot, especially if you're not sure if this is the final name you will use.

Tips:

1. Try to avoid generic names, for example, Charlie's Bar and Grill, Pete's Auto, Liz's Hair Salon etc. They're hard to remember and virtually impossible to trademark.

2. Try to avoid generic names that simply describe the product or service, for example, Great Hot Pizza or All Auto Repairs or Best Accounting and Book-keeping etc.

3. Be careful using geographical names, especially if you have plans to expand. Sacramento Auto repairs won't work outside Sacramento.

4. Try not to use a name that may go out of fashion or use. Bob's Horse and Buggy or Betty's Hula Hoops or Lake Tahoe Blacksmith's are names you could probably easily get now.

5. Try to keep the name short and easy to pronounce unless it adds cache, for example, Australian wines or New Zealand beer.

> **Brainstorm and write down the business names that come to mind for further research.**

Business Logo/Trademark

When you combine a brand with a business name and a logo you have three of the most powerful marketing pieces of a business. When a customer, employee, vendor, lender sees either one of them and they recognize it, you evoke an emotional response, be it good or bad. Deciding on a business logo may not be a quick process. Additionally, you may welcome professional help. My suggestion is to not rush into this piece if you don't have the time or can't find exactly what you want. As your business starts and evolves, ideas will come to you. Once you get a number of ideas, explore each of these further until you find the perfect fit. As I've said, this may involve hiring a professional to help you with this. You can spend the money now if you think there is a critical need and you will get a return on investment, but if your business idea is gaining traction in the market and the customer base is changing, it may be too early to decide on that perfect business logo. I recently heard one of the executives of Nike say that they paid a graphic designer about $200 to come up with the Nike swoosh. Nike now spend billions of dollars promoting that swoosh so there is the importance of the business logo.

College students doing graphic arts are a great source of ideas. A couple of websites that allow you to post an ad for help designing a business logo include Craigslist (www.craigslit.com), eLance (www.elance.com) or Buyer Zone (www.buyerzone.com).

Elements of a Business Logo

There are essentially two elements to a business logo:

Size

Whatever image you decide to settle on, make sure it is scalable. Being scalable means it looks fine on a business card which is obviously small, and still meets your "lookability" test when you transfer it to a poster or banner to use in a trade show or a sign for the front of your business if you have a retail location.

Colors

You may be tempted to use a rainbow of colors in your business logo so it stands out. That's a nice idea that your commercial printer will love as each time you have something printed it's going to cost more. Keep your logo to one or two colors as this will be your lowest cost. You can always shade the same color if you want the contrast of more than one color, for example, if you want red and black and a third color you could use grey which is a shade of black. Don't think two colors are restrictive. Some of the best business logos are two colors. For example, Coca-Cola, Kraft, Heinz, Exxon etc.

Trademark

If you have the perfect business logo and don't want others to use it or copy it, you can register it as a trademark. For more information about how to do this, go to Page 56 and it will give you the contact details for the **U.S. Patent & Trademark Office.**

Take out a pencil and start making some creative logos. While you are brainstorming think about key words or business names you would like to use.

Elevator Speech

So what's an elevator speech? Imagine you walk into the first floor of an elevator and you push the tenth floor button. You see the third floor button's been pushed and so you turnaround to see the person and the person you see is one of the most important people you would like to meet. The first thing you would probably think of doing is getting off at the third floor but you've pushed the tenth floor button. So you need to find a way between the first floor and the third floor (about 15 to 30 seconds) to convince that person that they need to spend more time with you, preferably with a second meeting so you can really explain what it is that you have to say. So that's an elevator speech. The ability to convert a first time contact with somebody into a second meeting or appointment by having something specific and universal to say under any situation. In simple terms, you need an advertisement about you and your business to knock their socks off in the shortest time possible.

Critically – make it short, simple and memorable and rehearse it thoroughly so it sounds natural and not contrived.

Sample elevator pitches:

"I'm the owner of an auto body shop in North Highlands called Sam's. It's a new business and if your car breaks down and needs repair we do all the work for you and provide a free rental until it's fixed. I also service all American made cars and guarantee to have the job finished the same day as long as the car is at my business by 8.00 am."

"I'm a business broker and have owned five businesses. All my discussions with you are totally confidential. Before I list a business for sale I do a Brokers Opinion of Value so you can decide if the valuation price is right or not. My cost includes advertising the business on 41 websites and I am only paid if your business successfully sells. My qualifications include being a Certified Business Broker."

Write some sample elevator speeches in pencil so you can tweak and change. Once you get the one you like, commit it to memory and practice it in front of a mirror until it becomes natural.

Other Sales And Marketing Strategies, Tools And Ideas

With each of the five businesses I've owned and operated, one of the most difficult pieces has been the sales and marketing. I've found this the most difficult because I was so energized by my new business opportunity that I wanted to let everyone know I was open for business, but at the same time there were so many things to do to run the business, that I simply couldn't get them all done no matter how many hours I worked.

My suggestion as you start your business would be to ask yourself some key questions. These are:
1. What is my strength – running the management side of the business or doing sales and marketing?
2. Where do I get the most Return-On-Investment – running the management side of the business or doing sales and marketing?
3. What do I enjoy doing the most – management or sales and marketing?
4. Do I know a better manager or salesperson who could do either task for me and would I be better to hire them?

I expect you will do what I ended up doing with my first four businesses, and that was to do it all myself. If that's what you decide, my final suggestion would be to keep it simple. There are so many sales and marketing things you can do. I believe you will make the mistake of wasting time and money if you try to do too many things, as each needs to be measured to see if it is working. If you have too many things you are trying to do, you will spread yourself too thin, and not use your time and money wisely.

Below is a list of sales and marketing ideas you can try. There are many more but each take learning, testing, monitoring and time to find what fits your business best, so don't overinvest in any one area until you truly know it works.

- ✓ Direct mail
- ✓ Telemarketing
- ✓ Yellow Pages advertising
- ✓ Tombstone ads
- ✓ Public Speaking
- ✓ Seminars
- ✓ Newsletters
- ✓ Electronic newsletters
- ✓ Tags attached to your email signature
- ✓ Postcards
- ✓ Flyers
- ✓ Inserts in newspapers
- ✓ Radio advertising
- ✓ Radio shows
- ✓ Teleclasses or teleseminars over the internet
- ✓ Networking
- ✓ Trade shows
- ✓ Press releases
- ✓ Drop cards
- ✓ Website
- ✓ Electronic newsletters
- ✓ Lunch with key customers

- ✓ Preferred Partner relationships – working with non competitors but people who have a product or service that is complementary to you.
- ✓ Make a donation to local charities and schools
- ✓ Discount coupons
- ✓ Pennysaver magazines
- ✓ In-home parties
- ✓ Craigslist
- ✓ Magnets/Pens and similar give-aways

Don't forget there is a cost both in time and money to do ANY of these activities. Money will invariably be limited so tie whatever you do into both your Startup Expenses spreadsheet and Sales and Marketing budget.

For more information on different sales and marketing strategies visit the web. A great website for ideas is www.businessinfoguide.com

5 Components Of A Successful Sales And Marketing Plan

A sales and marketing plan can be strategic or tactical. It depends on its audience, the complexity of the business, and the purpose of the document. For a business starting out, I suggest you keep it as simple as possible and record different sales and marketing activities you hear and see that you want to try some time. If you try too many options starting out you will spend too much money, waste too much time, and confuse yourself trying to learn too much at the expense of other things you should focus on.

A good sales and marketing plan when written in detail includes the following:

1. Write this section about your product or service so it's clear what you are offering and why customers would want to do business with you. Focus on the 4 P's. Product, Price, Promotion, Place.
2. Get some feedback from non threatening people or groups before going to market who may buy your product or service. You want to know what they think personally and what they think is important to the market. Know and explain - who are you selling to? What do your customers want? What is your USP? (Unique Selling Position). Which marketing tactics will give your product or service prominence not only in its own right but against your competitors. When, how often and at what cost will you use your marketing strategies? Where do you want your business to be in 12 months?
3. Now take your idea to market and get direct feedback by listening to actual customers. Once you have enough data do a SWOT analysis – Strengths, Weaknesses, Opportunities, Threats.
4. Draft the plan so you have written details about what you want to do and how you are doing it.
5. Track the results to know what is and isn't working so you can go back to 2 above and work through the plan by doing it all over again and again.

Finally, don't rest on your laurels. Markets change all the time and you must be ready. Make sure to review the plan every year to see if you must revisit any goals.

Sales And Marketing Plan

If you would like to create a sales and marketing plan and put it in writing, below is a suggested outline. The main strategy to follow is to have the Sales and Marketing Plan work in conjunction with the Business Plan and the Productivity Plan (which we will talk about shortly.) I do think it's a great idea to put your plan into a written document as this process makes you focus and work through the variables. Plus once it's written down it's so easy to go back and review it and make changes as necessary.

Sales and Marketing Plan outline:

1. Executive Summary

The easiest strategy for creating the Executive Summary is to simply take it from the business plan. It can also be a fresh document, the choice is yours.

a. Description of the Company

The company description includes a brief history such as when it was founded, and general information about the current owners of the business. Keep it simple and to about 10 lines.

b. Vision Statement

If the company has one, simply place it here. A good vision statement shouldn't need explanation. A very brief history about how the vision statement was chosen can be included, if necessary.

c. Mission Statement

Same as the Vision Statement. Drop it in here and move on. The mission statement should be included on all marketing plans.

d. Products and Services

A very brief description of the company's products and services. If the sales and marketing plan is internal and won't go to a lender or used by another company unfamiliar with the business then no detailed explanation is required. If this document can go to external customers or vendors then a brief explanation of the main products and services is a good idea.

e. Financial Feasibility

This section should also come straight from the business plan and give a brief description of the financial outlook of the industry and the company, and what effects may arise if the marketing is not successful. Don't discuss financial plans for the marketing program in this section of the document.

2. Strategic Focus and Plan

a. Mission/Vision

This is the place to state what you would like out of the marketing plan. If this is a marketing plan for a single product, then this statement should state what your company expects out of the product and how they plan to achieve the goals.

b. Objectives

The objectives of the marketing for the particular product, service or company should be outlined in this section. If one of the objectives is to make 50,000 people aware of your new product then this is something that should be included in your objectives. You can also include company objectives in this section if they are directly affected by your marketing. For instance, if your goal is to make one million dollars in sales the first year, then this is an objective that comes in direct contact with the marketing program.

c. Competitive Environment

Companies don't exist in a vacuum. They have competition. Outline the competitive environment of your product, market or service. This would include any competitors whether they are in direct or indirect competition.

d. Situation Analysis

A good marketing tool that outlines the products and their effectiveness is a SWOT Analysis. SWOT stands for Strengths, Weakness, Opportunities and Threats. On page 155 we show a SWOT template. Review this model and process and include it in your Sales and Marketing report to bring clarity.

e. Competitive Analysis

This section differs from the competitive environment as it describes more in-depth how you plan to effectively market against the competition. This section should outline direct competition's weaknesses, and how you plan to capitalize on these weaknesses to grab the market share.

3. Market Product Focus

a. Marketing Objectives

Your marketing objectives can take one of two formats; strategic or tactical. If the marketing plan is to outline all objectives of the company you would write strategic objectives. You could list these in numerical order and explain in detail how those objectives are to be accomplished.
Should the plan be for a specific product or service it would be tactical. Use the same number and descriptive format but instead this time explain the objective and tie it in to the strategic sales and marketing plan so the reader can see what is to be accomplished.

b. Target Markets

All products and services are created to meet the demand of a target market or markets. Use this section to define in detail the market in which you will be marketing your product. Describe in detail the target market(s) and outline your conclusions. Clearly state why this market is going to use your product or service and support your argument with the research that's been done to arrive at this conclusion.

4. Marketing Program

a. Product Strategy

If you are selling a product, outline the strategy you will use for this product with a detailed description of your product(s) are and how they are going to benefit your company. If you are doing an individual product marketing plan, then this section would describe in detail what your product is and what strategies you have to make it beat out your competitors.

b. Price Strategy

The price strategy is where you will describe your key pricing issues. It is a good idea to state whether you are taking the high cost/low turnover method or the low cost/high turnover method. If you think your key selling point is going to be the price, then explain that here. If you are taking the low cost/high turnover approach, then explain how your company will succeed with the low profit margin on each product. Be sure to include rough estimates of profit margins, manufacturing costs and end consumer prices.

c. *Promotion Strategy*

The promotion strategy is one of the most important sections of the marketing plan. This is where it can make or break a marketing program. This section should include advertising strategies you plan to engage in, any marketing strategies for your products such as attending trade shows, conferences etc. Also you should explain what message you want to promote in all of the items mentioned above. You should send the same message through all channels of communication.

Get on with it!!

Now that you have your plan, go out and make it real. There is no use spending months in analysis paralysis trying to write a perfect plan. Rather, have a bias towards action and go get started NOW.

Importance of your sales and marketing plan

The Sales and Marketing plan ties in with the Business Plan and argues the method to attract new customers, keep the existing customers, and thereby grow the business. It also focuses on the product or service(s) you are offering, and what research has been done to support the premise that there is a market for the product, and that market will allow you to build and deploy your product or service and at the end of the day, not only cover your costs but make a profit.

From my perspective, the better the Life Plan, Business Plan, Sales and Marketing Plan and Productivity Plan are all tied in together AND communicated to the employees so they understand their role, the more successful the business will be. If the economy is struggling, then the impact may not be obvious but you will be doing things your competitors are not doing. Use these different plans you make to give your business foundation and direction, and success will come to you.

Productivity Plan

Most business owners are familiar with the idea of a business plan and possibly a sales and marketing plan. From the work I do as a Business Broker it is easy to see that most small business owners don't have a business plan nor indeed a sales and marketing plan. I suspect the reasons include they do not have the time to create the document, see little value in spending the time to start it as they are not sure when they will need it, or simply don't know how to use it effectively.

The true value of a business plan is that it forces ideas or more specifically, goals, to be written down on paper. As business owners, we carry ideas in our head and because we live and breathe the business think we have its direction is under control. I suspect this is far from the truth. As the saying goes, if you fail to plan, you plan to fail.

So here's the solution.

The Business plan is the strategic vision and direction of the business. This should be a living and breathing document that is constantly changed. The sales and marketing plan is a subset of the business plan in that it defines how customers are created, kept, and maintained. Again, this should be a living and breathing document. From my perspective, the document missing that truly brings the business plan and sales and marketing plan together is the productivity plan.

A productivity plan is the tasks that need to be completed on either a daily, weekly or monthly basis. These tasks can be divided into basic operations to marketing and sales activities; whatever flows from the business and sales and marketing plans.

Use your plan to get the most out of each work day.

Create your plan

The productivity plan applies at the individual level by defining tasks and goals to achieve. If there are particular tasks you need to complete each week to achieve that goal, designate a specific day of the week to accomplish this task. For example, you might conduct a team meeting on Mondays, schedule one-on-one time with key employees on Tuesdays, review financial statements on Wednesdays, and so on.

Assigning important tasks to a specific day of the week will help get you into a routine and minimize distractions or if your productivity plan gets full and the task you need done is important, you can delegate it and schedule a task to review the results with the person you delegated the task. Also, by breaking down tasks, it often creates a sub set of tasks all of which need to be done. For example, if your team meeting is planned for Monday you may need to create a subset of tasks such as getting a report completed by end of business Wednesday, on Thursday meeting with your sales and marketing person, phoning to get quotes on certain items, ordering a new piece of equipment etc and schedule training on it etc.

As you plan your productivity list, before accepting it, try to answer the following questions.

1. Will this task help me with my general organization?
2. Will this task improve the company's bottom line?
3. What tasks should I be doing that I tend to avoid?

4. Is this task part of my responsibilities or can it be delegated or outsourced for a cheaper cost than me doing it?

Here are some other ideas to stimulate your thoughts. These thoughts are sales and marketing centric so you can adapt these to different areas of the business such as management, finance, Human Resources etc.

1. Perform 10 cold calls today
2. Attend Wednesday evening networking event
3. Add a new page to the website or update an existing page
4. Submit an article to the local press
5. Attend a monthly webinar on the latest sales techniques
6. Meet weekly with a mentor
7. Read industry newsletters or magazines etc first thing Thursday morning
8. Speak in public on a monthly basis

Write your plan in either a word processing document or in a spreadsheet format, and update it regularly, preferably on the same computer as your business plan and sales and marketing plan so you can synchronize all of them. You could also consider printing it out and posting it near your desk so it's always handy. In addition to a weekly plan, you can also define monthly and yearly goals. Once you begin to check off tasks, not only will you feel a sense of accomplishment, but your productivity will inevitably improve.

Your plan doesn't have to stop with you. If you have employees or a virtual assistant, be sure to create plans for them too. Soon everyone in your business will be working smarter and your only regret will be that you didn't create your plans sooner.

Technology Plan

The idea of a technology plan may sound over the top for a business starting out. However, I think this is a critical topic for all businesses these days as technology is so immersed in all areas of any business. When you get your hair cut, the business has a computer system to record your home phone number and any other personal details you choose to give, the local restaurants provide electronic buzzers to alert you that your table is ready, the local mechanic has a system that records the work performed on your car, hotels and motels have international reservation systems plus the ubiquitous laptop computer follows us everywhere.

So what's a technology plan?

At its simplest level it's a place to record all the software you use, the username and passwords you need on so many websites, the short cuts you choose to forget on how to do certain things on certain websites, or software that you don't choose to remember because you last used it 4 months ago etc.

A technology plan can be as simple as that and then grow as the business grows. It can also be used to document the PC hardware you use including make, model, and serial numbers, vendors you use and interact with, other systems you interface with, tools you use such as webinars and other on-line meetings and PC tasks you need to address such as backups, software vendors, hardware vendors etc.

Bottom line – don't forget the importance of the technology you use and record as many details as you can as technology is supposed to work for you, not the other way round. Keep this file in a central location so if others need the information they can readily find it without having to try and get you out of a meeting or presentation you are doing with a customer.

Tax Minimization Plan

Possibly the most neglected and most misunderstood part of owning and operating a business is the part that concerns the payment of federal and state taxes or more accurately, the ability to pay the least amount of tax. This is especially true for startup businesses as in the formative years of the business, there may be little profit generating from the business, but if taxes need to be paid then the amount that's paid if it's not planned for, can disrupt the cash flow of the business, and thereby hold back the growth of the business.

There is no getting around preparing and lodging a tax return if you want to sleep at night and put your positive energy into running and growing your business. So what needs to be done is effective planning to minimize the tax to be paid when it becomes due.

It's not the goal of this guide or this section to cover all the tax minimization options. It couldn't be done. The goal here is simply to highlight the need for research and planning if you have the time, or alternatively getting professional advice.

The best way to achieve the above is part of your process of finding the right accountant or tax agent. In Section Two there is a section called Professionals you can hire and this outlines how to look for the right professional help.

The bottom line though is to ensure you plan for your tax responsibilities before they become due and payable. And as they are due and payable every year do the necessary planning. If you operate as a sole proprietor or have a corporation or company that has a calendar tax year, I would suggest you start looking at your tax responsibilities after Thanksgiving. If your company or corporation has a different tax year than December 31, put a note in your Business Plan to research your tax responsibilities about 6 weeks prior to the tax year expiring.

Finance Plan

Securing a loan can be a slow and frustrating process, so I if finance is needed by the buyer, this process should have been identified and begun some time ago. The process will vary depending on the type of loan required such as an SBA loan, or conventional loan, or maybe you are using a short term home equity loan. Regardless, before signing any final paperwork, check the status of your loan as it will give you a road map for making "go forward" decisions.

Write down questions about the financing process so you can check later.

Obtain Lender Instructions

As we just mentioned, when third party financing is involved, the lender will require a lot of documents. While most of these are provided by the buyer, the seller is also required to provide some documentation. As the process continues, the lender may request even more documents and more information. As the owner of the business, be patient with the process and supply all documents as quickly and readily as you can so the process keeps moving.

NOTE:

If a third party lender provides financing, the time to process all the paperwork and get approval can take anywhere from 30 to 60 days, with 45 days being about the norm. If the third party lender is a loan from the Small Business Administration, there are strict processes for the lender to follow with no shortcuts allowed. Bottom line: Respond as quickly and professionally as you can, otherwise you may end up killing the transaction.

Track requests you receive for seller documents:

What You Will Need To Get A Loan To Start Your Business

If you are serious about starting your business there are four things you will need to move through the process. You don't need to provide these to everybody that asks, but if you have them prepared and ready to go it will allow you to keep the momentum going. Plus these are documents that change so if you create an initial document it will be easy to update, when, and if necessary.

The documents you need are:

1. Resume

A resume is now an important component for three reasons. First, your resume talks about your industry experience. Second, your resume talks about your business and management experience and education. If you need to apply for finance, this is information a lender wants to know. Obviously the better and more qualified you are, the greater your chances are of getting that loan.

A resume may also be handy when applying for credit from suppliers. It's not necessary for smaller suppliers but if you want to get credit from a larger company, your resume speaks to your business and professional background.

2. Copy of your credit score

Yes – you guessed it. The same reason you need a credit score is the reasons outlined above. Also, my suggestion is that you pull your credit score and have it available to provide when you feel comfortable providing it. If your credit score is pulled too many times in a short period of time, it can lower your score. Plus, if you supply your credit score when you feel comfortable providing it, it puts you in control.

3. Personal Financial Statement

The need for a Personal Financial Statement mirrors the same reason you need a resume. Most lenders and suppliers want you to have a minimum net worth before approving a loan. Their goal is to understand your current level of business and personal debt so they can determine if they approve a loan to you that you'll have the ability to pay it back.

Below is a suggested template for showing your assets and liabilities. You can write in this template or if you prefer, I have a free Excel from SCORE you can download and use. To get this document, go to my website http://www.Andrew-Rogerson.com. On the left hand side of the Home Page there is a menu that includes one towards the bottom called Sample Documents. Click on this and once the page displays you will see different Word and Excel files created by SCORE. Document 5- Personal Financial Statement is the one you want. If you want to know how long it will take to pay back a loan, document 6 - Loan Amortization Schedule will help you with that. And by the way, you are welcome to use any of the other documents.

Financial Statement

ASSETS			LIABILITES & NET WORTH		
Cash In Banks (itemize)	$		Notes Due Banks and Others (itemized)	$	
	$			$	
	$			$	
Marketable Stocks & Bonds	$		Taxes Payable	$	
	$			$	
Life Insurance Cash Surrender Value	$		Loans	$	
	$			$	
TOTAL CURRENT ASSETS	$		TOTAL CURRENT LIABILITIES	$	
	$			$	
Real Estate Owned	$		Real Estate Mortgages	$	
Other Assets	$		Other Liabilities	$	
	$			$	
Retirement Accounts	$			$	
IRAs	$		TOTAL NON-CURRENT LIABILITIES	$	
401k	$		TOTAL LIABILITES	$	
TOTAL NON-CURRENT ASSETS	$		NET WORTH	$	
TOTAL ASSETS	$		TOTAL LIABILITES & NET WORTH	$	

SOURCE OF ANNUAL INCOME		ESTIMATE OF ANNUAL EXPENSES	
Salary		Mortgage Payments	
Bonus & Commissions		Automobile Payments or Lease	
Dividends		Insurance Premiums	
Other Income		Other Expenses	
TOTAL		TOTAL	

I certify that the information I have provided above is complete and correct. I only authorize the release of this information to obtain verification with written approval from me.

Yes – I agree ☐Name _____

4. Agreement with your significant other or partner

This last one was thrown in for good measure but it's probably the most important, but the least obvious. How does your wife, husband, significant other or partner feel about you starting a business? The industry you've chosen? Will they work in the business with you? Have you discussed the financial and emotional risks you are taking? The questions are endless. Make sure your partner travels with you on all aspects of this journey. Yes – two heads are better than one, but if you both work through the many variables it will help you both once you get into the actual process of opening and running your business. Also, as a business broker when I am consulting with buyers or sellers of a business I ALWAYS like the partner to attend any meetings so I can make sure there is agreement on any steps being taken and address any concerns together so if there are clarifying questions, both parties hear and are comfortable with any agreements. If they aren't on board with you, your chances of success are greatly diminished, plus it adds a great stress on your relationship.

Tasks Template

With lots to do and so little time, let's stay organized and focused on completing tasks as they apply to starting your business. Use the blank spaces to add the tasks as they apply to your business.

Task	Who completes	Target completion date	Date completed
Join a trade association or industry group			
Join a college class on a subject you want to learn about			
Read some general business books			
Subscribe to a trade magazine or newspaper			
Create your legal entity			
File a DBA			
Create a logo or business name or both			
Jot down some ideas for your life plan			
Write your business plan			
Pencil out a Vision Statement & Mission Statement			
Write your Sales and Marketing plan			
Create your Productivity plan			
Make a business startup budget			
Create a sales forecast spreadsheet			
Create a cash flow projection for 1st year			
Obtain a Federal ID #			
Obtain a business license			

Task	Who completes	Target completion date	Date completed
Find a mentor			
Create a personal financial statement			
Interview lenders about your finance needs			
Open a bank account for the business			
Look for office space or an Executive Suite			
Print some basic business stationary			
Apply for business licenses and permits			
Create an outline for an Operations Manual			
Create an outline for a Training Manual			
Create an outline for an Employee Manual			
Get costs and ideas on a website			
Register a domain name			
Talk to three competitors			
Inquire about insurances			
Get an accountant on your team			
Find the name of a good attorney			
Get business tools ready: PC, furniture, cash register etc			
Set the date to open your business			
Search the web for ideas and inspirations			
Update the Business Plan quarterly			

Task	Who completes	Target completion date	Date completed
Update the Sales & Marketing plan each quarter			

End Of Chapter Notes

Use this page to write down notes, ideas and other brainstorming for starting your business.

Let's get started

"Don't let what you cannot do interfere with what you can do."

John Wooden, Hall of Fame basketball coach

Introduction

Sections one and two of this guide provides some background information about starting a business. Section Three encourages you to plan and put structure into what you are doing in case you get somebody that wants to buy your business. The goal of this section is to take all the planning you have done and take your business into the market.

Assemble Your Team

The first step is to bring together the team you need to start your business. In Section Two we talked about the different professionals and their skills you can hire to help you. Now is the time to finalize the members of your team so you are ready to move forward.

To finalize the members of your team, you may like to go back and revisit the topic in Section Two called 'Professionals you can hire.' Your goal is to review your business plan and decide what professional help you need, if any, interview suitable candidates to ensure there is a match for you and the professional you wish to hire, and negotiate any costs involved.

Make your final selection on the basis that this will be a long term relationship. If a professional is not working for you there is no problem making a change; in fact it makes no sense other than to do that. The downside is that finding a replacement can take time and it may not be when you have downtime to do this, but need that service now, or it means you may lose momentum or the opportunity you have been waiting for.

To find the professionals you need the best place to start looking is with your immediate family and friends and people you trust. Your family and friends know you and what you're about and should be able to help and from their circle of influence suggest some people for you. If this doesn't address your need, there are some suggested places to go back in Section Two.

In deciding who these people should be, take into consideration:
1. The skills they bring; you don't want someone with the same skill set if it clashes with your own.
2. A skill set that compliments and complements your own skills and that you believe you are lacking. To be clear, it's important that when you hire somebody to work with you that your working relationship is relaxed. We all have our own personality, style, habits and ways of doing things. Because this is your business, make sure the person you hire understands how you work. It's their responsibility to adjust; not yours.
3. The amount of time they have to help you and whether they will be readily available.
4. The costs involved in hiring the experts you need.
5. Whether you like it or not, one of the most important skills you will want from these people is emotional support and empathy in that they understand what you are going through and their advice is in your best interest and your best interest only. But most important of all, you want someone that will give you an honest answer to tough questions.

Use the following chart to write down the names of primary and secondary people you need for your team.

Service required	Option 1	Option 2	Option 3
CPA/Accountant/Book-keeper			
Attorney			
Personal Financial Planner			
Marketing Consultant			
Mentor			

Once you build your team, try to avoid changing it.

Starting a business is a complicated process. If you surround yourself with good people and have a strong focus and clear focus on what you are doing, everyone understands your vision and culture and their role then hang on to them.

Value Of A Mentor

There's a great quote that goes something like this "If I was the sole source of inspiration for my business it would go broke." In very simple terms, one person cannot do it all. There are too many variables, quick and constant change, the need to have balance in our lives (hence my suggestion in Section Three to have a life plan)

A solution to the above is to find a mentor. Let me be a little clearer – the solution to the above is to find a good mentor that works for both of you. If you are lucky enough to find the right mentor then it can bring so many positive contributions to what you do.

8 tips to find a good mentor

1. Probably the two most important ingredients in a mentor relationship are integrity and character both couched in someone you respect and trust. Look for integrity and character and if that works, make sure there is respect and trust…in both directions.
2. Possibly the hardest part is finding someone interested in working with you as a mentor. They need to be open and willing to relate and work with you as the relationship should naturally involve discussing both professional and personal issues.
3. If the last point is challenging, the number one reason it can be hard to find the right mentor is that they simply lack the time. Try to find someone who has the time and the willingness to spend with you. This may take time but you'll have to be patient as the mentor relationship you seek is long term for a true mentor relationship to evolve and truly work. Part of your requirement is to be flexible and work in with your mentor's schedule.
4. A good question is whether to look for somebody in your industry or completely removed from it. The best option is to find somebody in the same or a similar industry who is not a competitor as this cuts down a lot of work explaining industry jargon and problems. However, the key is that the relationship works for both parties, so lack of industry knowledge can be overcome if the ingredients are right.
5. Similarly, don't be afraid to look beyond your neck of the woods. A person with an expertise in another discipline or field can provide new insights about different business principles, and provide a new perspective.
6. A word of caution. Your mentor will be human. A good mentor will provide new insights, but they won't solve all your personal or business problems. In fact, a good mentor will help you solve your own problems or if they feel it is necessary, direct you to another source for special problems.
7. Openness is one of the key ingredients to a mentor relationship. If you don't feel comfortable being open and honest with someone, then mentoring is not for you. A good mentor will let you into their world, sharing both professional and personal triumphs and failures.
8. Mentoring is a journey and takes time to evolve. As long as you're learning something you didn't know before, the mentoring relationship is working. Like all good things in life, it takes as long as it takes.

7 Stages Of The Business Life Cycle

As your business enters the market; and this may sound obvious, but be aware that the economy is already in motion and you will be joining it at a certain time in its evolution. If you are able to recognize what's happening, it will give you an insight about how your business is accepted and positioned, or more accurately, the product or service you are offering. Below are the 7 stages of a business life cycle. Be aware of these cycles as they will also influence many of the major decisions you make such as adding new hires, spending money on sales and marketing to grow the business, adding additional office or factory space to the business to grow it, to name a few examples.

1. Seed Stage:

The seed stage of your business life cycle is when your business is just a thought or an idea. This is the very conception or birth of a new business and where we are currently focused.
- ✓ Challenge: Most new businesses will have to overcome the initial challenge of market acceptance. A strategy for this situation would be to pursue one niche opportunity and be the best. That's where your business plan comes in as this will guide you. Do not spread money and time resources too thin.
- ✓ Focus: The focus for this stage of the business is on matching the business opportunity with your skills, experience, energy, and enthusiasm. Other focal points include deciding on a business ownership structure, finding professional advisors, and business planning.
- ✓ Money Sources: Early in the business life cycle with no proven market or customers, you will need to rely on your own cash or friends and family. Other potential sources include suppliers, customers, and government grants. Make sure you allocate time to uncover these funds.

2. Start-Up Stage:

Your business is born and now exists legally. Products or services are in production and you have your first customers.
- ✓ Challenge: If your business is in the start-up life cycle stage, it is likely you have overestimated money needs and the time to get to market. The main challenge is not to burn through what little cash you have. You need to learn what profitable needs your clients have and do a reality check to see if your business is on the right track.
- ✓ Focus: Start-ups require establishing a customer base and market presence along with tracking and conserving cash flow.
- ✓ Money Sources: Owner, friends, family, suppliers, customers, or grants.

3. Growth Stage:

Your business has made it through the toddler years and is now a child. Revenues and customers are increasing with many new opportunities and issues. Profits are strong, but competition is surfacing.
- ✓ Challenge: The biggest challenge for a growth company is dealing with the constant range of issues and their time and money demands. Strong management is required and a possible new business plan. Learn how to train and delegate to conquer this stage of development.
- ✓ Focus: Growth life cycle businesses are focused on running the business in a more formal way to deal with the increase in sales and customers. Better accounting and management systems need to be set-up. New employees will have to be hired to deal with the influx of business.
- ✓ Money Sources: Banks, profits, partnerships, grants and leasing options.

4. Established Stage:

Your business has now matured into a thriving company with a place in the market and loyal customers. Sales growth is not explosive but manageable. Business life now becomes more routine.

- ✓ Challenge: It is far too easy to rest on your laurels during this life stage. You have worked hard and have earned a rest, but the marketplace is relentless and competitive. Stay focused on the bigger picture. Issues like the economy, competitors or changing customer tastes can quickly end all the hard work you've done.
- ✓ Focus: An established life cycle company will be focused on improvement and productivity. To compete in an established market, you will require better business practices along with automation and outsourcing to improve productivity.
- ✓ Money Sources: Profits, banks, investors, and government.

5. Expansion Stage:

This phase is characterized by a period of growth into new markets and distribution channels. This stage is often the choice of the small business owner to gain a larger market share and find new revenue and profit channels.
- ✓ Challenge: Moving into new markets requires the planning and research of a seed or start-up stage business. Focus should be on businesses that complement your existing experience and capabilities. Moving into unrelated businesses can be disastrous.
- ✓ Focus: Add new products or services to existing markets or expand existing business into new markets and customer types.
- ✓ Money Sources: Joint ventures, banks, licensing, new investors and partners.

6. Decline Stage:

Changes in the economy, society, or market conditions can decrease sales and profits. This may quickly end many small companies.
- ✓ Challenge: Businesses in the decline stage of the life cycle will be challenged with dropping sales, profits, and negative cash flow. The biggest issue is how long the business can support a negative cash flow. Ask is it time to move on to the final life cycle stage...exit.
- ✓ Focus: Search for new opportunities and business ventures. Cutting costs and finding ways to sustain cash flow are vital for the declining stage.
- ✓ Money Sources: Suppliers, customers, owners.

7. Exit Stage:

This is the big opportunity for your business to cash out on all the effort and years of hard work. Or it can mean shutting down the business.
- ✓ Challenge: Selling a business requires your realistic evaluation. It may have been years of hard work to build the company, but what is its real value in the current market place.
- ✓ Focus: Get a proper valuation on your company. Look at your business operations, management and competitive barriers to make the company worth more to the buyer. Set-up legal buy-sell agreements along with a business transition plan.
- ✓ Money Sources: Find a business valuation partner. Consult with your accountant and financial advisors for the best tax strategy to sell or close down the business.

Each stage of the business life cycle may not occur in chronological order. Some businesses will be "built to flip"; quickly going from start-up to exit. Others will choose to avoid expansion and stay in the established stage.

Whether your business is a glowing success or a dismal failure depends on your ability to adapt to its changing life cycles. What you focus on and overcome today will change in the future. Understanding where your business fits on life cycle will help you foresee upcoming challenges and make the best business decisions. This may include accepting an offer should the right buyer come along.

Test The Market

Not every new business needs to test the market with their new service or product, but if this is an option and it's done properly, it will certainly provide great feedback and add considerably to the chances of the business being successful.

While you are developing your product or service it's a good idea to keep testing the market to make sure you are still on the right track. You can do this by using:

Focus groups

Ask small groups of your target customers what they want from your product or service. Make sure you create a consistent set of questions that are asked under the same conditions.

Questionnaires or surveys

If done properly, questionnaires and surveys can be a great means of getting feedback. The trick is to try and get as wide a sample as possible.

Prototypes

Consider showing an early version of your product to customers. You may find that your prototype will go through several stages of development as you refine your idea.

You may need to respond to suggestions from customer by modifying what you do. Don't be discouraged, as this is the very reason you are testing the market. Entrepreneurs do not view this as a failure, but as a learning curve.

If you are making a product, consider sending it to a large or very reputable organization. A positive testimonial will prove invaluable as you approach other customers.

You may want to consider testing even after your product goes on sale. Ongoing contact with customers can uncover both the shortcomings of your product, and possible opportunities that you may have missed.

Once you have a final product, you can then set about building a brand. A brand includes everything that is visible to the customer, such as the product name, its packaging and its delivery.

You also need to consider your pricing policy. You need to price all the materials, other inputs, machinery, processes and administrative time realistically. You will need to research different suppliers and the cost of marketing and distribution. Then check on the price at which your competitors are selling to customers. You can determine the price of your product or service so that it is attractive to customers and you make a profit.

Kaizen – Continuous Improvement

There is no question that getting a business started and running takes a lot of work. Once you get it to a certain level the temptation is to ease back and get it into maintenance mode while you work out the next direction for the business. Some of my suggestions in this guide have been to start your business and use the mindset discipline of making your decisions on the premise that a willing buyer is just around the corner.

As part of the culture you establish in your business, continuous improvement should always be part of it. Accepting mediocrity or second best permeates through a business and can prove fatal, so actively walk the talk and lead by example on "high standards" is a necessity from the leaders in the business. To help do this, consider using a continuous improvement methodology that becomes the normal culture of the business. There are different models to choose – Six Sigma, Lean and my personal preference is Kaizen but at a simple level.

Japanese companies incorporate Kaizen as part of their culture and it focuses on 5 premises. Briefly, these are:

1. Teamwork
2. Personal discipline
3. Improved morale
4. Quality circles
5. Suggestions for improvement

There are other components to Kaizen. If you have an interest to learn more, simply Google – "What is Kaizen?" and you will get plenty of results.

The simple point I leave here, and I mentioned it in Section Two, is that, in my opinion, a good business has ethics and culture. As the owner of the business and the one with the vision, creativity and leadership responsibility, you must choose what your business is about, what it stands for and how the community and market perceive it. If you agree business requires discipline and hard work, why not embrace those traits as you operate the business on a day to day basis as it will bring more and better custom, eliminate waste, and flow through to your bottom line.

It's All About Focus And Planning

As you work through the variables for deciding whether starting your business is right for you, here are some tips and encouragement.

Start with a strong focus and don't deviate until you have good foundations

Any new business has to be related to your own personal core competencies. This is the reason I make my suggestion that you find and follow your gift rather than your passion. Your gift will hold you in good stead whereas your passion may wane. Find what you're good at and what you enjoy doing and then it will not seem like work.

Secure a Client and Proceed with Confidence

Hewlett Packard is an example of an excellent company that allows its suppliers to have more than one customer. Some large technology companies want you to be their primary customer so when their business gets tough they can come back to you and demand lower prices or whatever they need. One of the keys to starting your business is to try and have one good customer…just to get started. Don't over-rely on that one customer, as your business can disappear if they are challenged or one of your competitors takes your place.

Test Your Market

When you start your new business it will be natural to have slow growth. Take advantage of this situation two ways. First, test the product or service you are providing to see its acceptance and popularity by getting first-hand feedback from the market. Second, as the business grows, survey your customers to find out what you are doing well and why (so you can market and promote the positive) and also find out what you are not doing so well so that can be improved.

Incidentally, if you have fast growth that too can be a problem as you may not have the money to fund the purchase of the materials, trained employees, office or warehouse size etc to sustain the business. But that's another story and a good one to have.

Make Sure You Have Enough Money

The number one reason new businesses fail is because they run out of money. Before starting your business work the numbers. Go back to Section Two and look at the topic called Budgets and other financial planning tools. Make sure you've built a personal budget for the next 12 months, a sales forecast for the next 12 months and 3 years, a break-even analysis and/or cash flow projection. Obviously they require a little work but they will give you a road map so you can know how you are performing. If tweaking is required, you'll know. If you aren't doing as well as expected you can sty making adjustments till things get where they need to be. Be a realist by looking at the worst case scenario which may be that you're not going to instantly get rich.

Get Support

When you start a new business there is so much to do and you are the center of it all. Therefore a couple of suggestions. First, don't forget you need downtime to think so you make good decisions. Try to find a club or association of like-minded people so you can mix with them and see your problems are not unique to you. Second, look for a mentor you can build a long term relationship with who can advise you on problems and hopefully put things into perspective, if that's what's needed. Always look out for more resources, they are available. Chambers of Commerce, Networking groups such as TNI and BNI, Meetup groups, Trade Associations, service groups such as Rotary, Kiwanis and Toastmasters to name a few.

Plan for Your Growth

This is such an important topic that I will mention it again. You must at least have a Business Plan complemented with a sales and marketing plan. If these plans are put to work and they generate results you will hopefully soon outgrow the space where you started. Bottom line – plan for growth by avoiding long term contracts. If you start your business from home and need additional office space, go to an Executive Suite. Executive Suites allow you to rent on a month to month basis and offer services such as telephone answering, mail delivery, secretarial services such as word processing, spreadsheet creation, desk top publishing etc. Once you've outgrown your Executive Suite service, look at renting your own office space but keep your lease duration manageable so there are not huge penalties if you need to find larger space again.

Use Effective Marketing

If sales and marketing is not your primary skill, go slow and carefully with it. Lots of money can be quickly and easily wasted thinking this direct mail campaign or telemarketing campaign or postcard mail out, or full page ad in the Yellow Pages will be a huge success. The bottom line is that sales and marketing is hit and miss; it is not a science. You have to try something specific and then tweak it and then tweak it again. Be patient and spend your money wisely and look for help from professionals, or attend networking groups to find out what's effective. As mentioned previously, testing a market is a great strategy. Be patient with it and analyze the results so you continually improve. From my perspective, marketing is a journey – not a destination. And don't forget the most powerful of all marketing – word of mouth.

Build a scalable business

Something a lot of new business owners do when starting out is jump into their passion or gift and start building their business to find they are the business. That is, all the customers and suppliers only want to talk to one person and that's you. So two suggestions. First, make sure the business you start can be serviced by employees and not just you. If your business isn't scalable you will almost definitely not find a buyer. The buyer will correctly deduce that all the knowledge is in your head, customers come to you because of you and your personality, and therefore it's too risky to try and buy that business from you.

10 Tips For A Successful Business Startup

Here are 10 tips to make sure your business start up is successful. In no particular order they are:

1. Undercapitalization

There's a quote that travel agents give to their customers when they are setting of on a trip and it goes like this. "Halve your luggage and double your money." The point is simple, far too many small business owners underestimate how much money they're going to need, not merely to get the business up and running, but also to sustain it as it struggles to gain a commercial foothold. That's part of the reason why they are small business owners. Lack of capital or more importantly a good use of the limited capital can restrict the growth and potential of the business.

2. Good Cash flow

If your business will provide credit to your customers, make sure the Accounts Receivables are managed closely. If your business is just starting out, consider setting your prices and include a discount for cash or payment up front rather than on credit. Cash is king. Cash flow is crucial to your success. Even businesses that move past the embryonic stage often collapse when incoming cash doesn't at least offset expenses and other costs.

3. Adequate Funding

This suggestion is similar to the first two but I've put it in here to underscore each of the above points and this one. Most small businesses fail because they do not have enough funding and the critical reason why 1 and 2 above become a problem. It gets back to one of my favorite mantra – if you fail to plan you plan to fail. It's important to create a comprehensive business plan as early as possible and include sales and marketing plans, growth strategies, budget planning, and an array of other elements.

4. Define a competitive edge or USP

Unique ideas are rare. It is critical that your business identify and latch onto a toehold in some sort of singular niche that you can exploit and claim as your own or as a Unique Selling Proposition (USP). This can mean making or providing a slight variation of the product or customer support that goes beyond your competitors and denotes you as an "expert" in that field. If you can position yourself as an expert it sets you apart from your competitors – a great place to be.

5. Strong and effective sales and marketing

It's essential to develop a strong sales and marketing plan that strategically identifies not only the business and who might come to use your product or service, but why. Make certain your marketing strategy sets you apart so a customer can clearly see why they would rather go to you than a competitor.

6. Remain flexible

Never forget to remain flexible. Providing a product and in particular a service means being as flexible and adaptable as you can. If a product isn't quite right or a marketing campaign isn't really flying, don't be afraid to make changes. To the contrary, it's critical that you do.

7. Be ready to over-deliver

Make sure you and your team focus on complete customer support, from doing things you don't have to, to offering thoughtful, useful advice that goes beyond the ordinary.

8. Set the standard high.

You've heard the expression; "Don't try to be all things to all people." An adaption for business would be "Don't try to be all things to all customers." Some customers with the product or service you provide will not be happy. You can try to focus on these or you can try to focus on over delivering to those that do like what you offer. As your business grows it's prudent to widen the net to try and be more things to more people, but don't try and do it from day one as you won't have enough resources to be successful.

9. Lead by example

Whether you like it or not, your values, attitude, communication style and other personal attributes will constantly be measured by your team. If you have a bad day and it becomes a frequent event, the attitude in your business is that bad days are acceptable. Make certain your employees are well-trained, fairly compensated, and understand your vision, and buy into it.

10. Early uncontrolled growth

This may seem ironic, but a small business can succeed too quickly pushing itself into an early grave or simply having to be sold. Make sure your production keeps pace with demand, or necessary expansion coincides with sufficient cash to fund it. The growth you dream about as an entrepreneur can actually threaten your business' very existence. Again, cover foreseeable growth in your business plan and track it with good book-keeping to make certain that it is managed successfully.

Grand Opening

If you're starting a new business and are opening your doors for the first time, it's a big event. This doesn't matter if your business is online, alongside a major freeway or tucked away in a remote industrial or commercial site. Your opening is cause for celebration because of all the work you've done getting to this point plus you need to introduce your business to the world so they know you are now open for business.

As you've been putting your business plan together and start up budget, hopefully it has included money to spend on your grand opening. Put planning, money, and energy into creating as much profile as you can. Ideas include:

- ✓ Ask everybody you've sought help or advice from to attend.
- ✓ Consider having the event catered so you can focus on meeting those that attend.
- ✓ Try to tie whatever you're doing with the business you're opening. If it's a food business, prepare and serve as much food as possible. If it's a printing business, hand out plenty of samples and a cross section of work to show what you do. Be creative to gain profile.
- ✓ Use invitations with an RSVP to invite as many people as possible.
- ✓ Decorate the location you will operate from so potential customers in the area now know you are open. If you are in a strip mall invite the other businesses.
- ✓ Consider partnering with other businesses that would benefit from your business. For example, a paper merchant with a printing business.
- ✓ Contact your suppliers you will be buying things from to see if they can give you free items or heavily discounted items you can use to gain visibility of your business.
- ✓ Consider a theme that complements your business. If it's a travel agency and its summer dress in Hawaiian attire.
- ✓ Consider formal invitations if that relates to the type of business you are opening.
- ✓ Contact your local media to see if they will promote your opening. A new business is a positive news story.
- ✓ Invite local business people you haven't met but would like to meet.
- ✓ Invite all your family and friends so you can say thank you to them for their help, but also have as many people attend as possible.
- ✓ Ask your family and friends to bring their family and friends. The more the merrier.
- ✓ Consider as many door prize(s) as possible so as many people as possible remember going to your new business location positively.
- ✓ Use music to add to the event. Try to relate the music to your type of business.
- ✓ If it's a family type business, have something for the children to do and make sure you advertise this so families know they are welcome and treat it as a night out for all their family.
- ✓ Use decorations to add to the event.
- ✓ Give everybody enough notice so they can plan to attend. A week's notice isn't long enough – 4 weeks is more appropriate – even longer. The longer your time the more people will talk about it and remember your business is now open.
- ✓ Don't worry about timing the Grand Opening to being the first day you open. In fact, consider a "soft" opening where you charge prices so you can "test" everything you do and iron out the wrinkles. Your Grand Opening can then be used to go to your normal prices.
- ✓ Your Grand Opening can go over a weekend or a week or a month. It doesn't need to be one day. If it goes longer than a weekend try to have different things happen at different times so customers come back and build the habit of coming to your business instead of to one of your competitors.

Tasks Template

In the previous section we provided this task list. You still have lots to do with little time but keep this list refreshed as it will give you a sense of accomplishment and keep you focused. Even put it into a Word or Excel file so you can regularly update it and see where you are at.

Task	Who completes	Target completion date	Date completed
Join a trade association or industry group			
Join a college class on a subject to learn about			
Read some general business books			
Subscribe to a trade magazine or newspaper			
Create your legal entity			
File a DBA			
Create a logo or business name or both			
Jot down some ideas for your life plan			
Write your business plan			
Pencil out Vision and & Mission Statements			
Write your Sales and Marketing plan			
Create your Productivity plan			
Make a business startup budget			
Create a sales forecast spreadsheet			
Create a cash flow projection for 1st year			
Obtain a Federal ID #			
Obtain a business license			
Find a mentor			

Task	Who completes	Target completion date	Date completed
Create a personal financial statement			
Interview lenders about your finance needs			
Open a bank account for the business			
Look for office space or an Executive Suite			
Print some basic business stationary			
Apply for business licenses and permits			
Create an outline for an Operations Manual			
Create an outline for a Training Manual			
Create an outline for an Employee Manual			
Get costs and ideas on a website			
Register a domain name			
Talk to three competitors			
Inquire about insurances			
Hire an accountant			
Find a good attorney			
Get business tools ready: PC, furniture, cash register etc			
Set the date to open your business			
Search the web for ideas and inspirations			
Update the Business Plan quarterly			
Update the Sales & Marketing plan quarterly			

End Of Chapter Notes

Use this page to write down notes, ideas and other brainstorming for starting your business.

Section Five

Getting and staying buyer ready

"For true success ask yourself the following four questions: Why? Why not? Why not me? Why not me, now?"

James Allen

Introduction

One of the main premises behind this guide is that if you decide to start your own business, always have it operating so it can be acquired by a buyer, if at that point in time this is what you would like to do.

There is great value in bringing this approach to starting your business. First, it makes have the records and processes in place that a buyer wants to see. Second, this discipline of starting the business and having it ready to be bought, requires you to run the business as all businesses should be – with discipline and with an eye on best practices. As a business broker I see so many businesses that have been successful, but that have lost their edge because the owners of the business have lost the drive and enthusiasm they once had and now a competitor, be it a larger player or an innovator are taking business from this company. Third, starting a business is a completely different skill and mind set to running a business on an everyday basis. Starting a business requires energy, a sense of urgency, creativity, a higher level of risk taking, vision, and other skills that are not always part of or encouraged in an established company which tends to be slower moving and process driven. For this reason, some entrepreneurs prefer the dynamic of starting their own business and then letting it be bought so they can do something else. The alternative thought here is that when the business reaches a level of success, it could be time to franchise or license the operation of the business to take it to the next level. If this is the next journey for the business, following the disciplines and structure I have been suggesting means the business is ready to present itself to lenders and equity partners to invest and grow the business.

The purpose of this section is to provide a brief overview of the key elements when selling a business. Knowledge is power, so understanding and being comfortable with these concepts will make it so much easier should you be approached by a buyer to acquire the business you started.

Understanding The Valuation Process

One of the first things you'll need to do if you have a buyer show interest in buying your business is get a valuation – of all components of the business. The type of valuation you need will be a function of the type of business. The normal process is to reach for a business appraiser. However, there are instances where it may be appropriate to get a Machinery and Equipment appraisal as the assets of the business are higher than the value the business generates. Additionally, if the business includes property, a commercial real estate appraisal will be necessary. There is a lot of information available on this topic but here are immediate considerations:
1. Beware of the scams.
2. Valuations or appraisals could be required for different parts of the business and they are rarely done by the same appraiser as they each have specialized training. You may need four valuations for the one business and here's why. If the business is a regular trading entity then you could get a business valuation. If the same business includes land and buildings you will need a commercial or property appraiser to do this for you. If the business includes a large amount of fixtures, furniture, electronic and/or machinery and equipment, you may need a Machinery and Equipment Appraiser (of which I am one.) If the business includes valuable intangible items such as trademarks, copyrights and/or patents, you would want an Intellectual Property appraisal.

Beware of Scams

Just so you are aware, there is a cottage industry of sales people calling on business owners and selling a business valuation—sometimes with an open listing agreement. These sales people offer to do a valuation of the business generally for a high fee—anywhere from $5,000 to $30,000 and more.

As an inducement to get the fee for the valuation, these sales people offer to take an open listing. This means the owner of the business is free to find their own buyer. However, the sales person offers to advertise and bring qualified buyers (or part of the pitch is that they already have them) and then receive a commission only if the business sells. The business owner thinks this is reasonable for three reasons:

First, the business owner needs a valuation and they are not sure how this is done. Second, the sales person only gets paid a commission if the business sells, and third, the sales person says he/she has a buyer.

There are two indicators that this is a scam. The first is that the price the business owner pays for the valuation is very high. Second, the sales person suggests their company has a lot of interested buyers and they have a great chance of bringing a qualified buyer to the business owner, when in fact this is highly unlikely.

Some clues that this may not be as good as it seems, are that the sales person is either from out of state or they are passing through the area and will not be back for a long period of time. Plus, the sales people tend to use pressure tactics and threats like: "If you are not interested, I will go to your competitor just down the road."

Types of Valuation

Business valuations can be very complex. It is critical for a professional business appraiser to understand the purpose of the valuation.

There are three types of valuations:
1. A Brokers Opinion of Value—Costs from $500 to $1,000 depending on the complexity.
2. A Standard Valuation—Costs from $3,000 to $5,000 depending on the structure of the business, the reason, and complexity of the valuation.
3. A Full Appraisal—Costs from $7,500 for complex valuations that do or may involve litigation.

To help understand valuations it is necessary to understand Uniform Standards of Professional Appraisal Practice (USPAP). USPAP sets the generally accepted standards for professional appraisal practices in North America, similar in purpose to GAAP which is used by the accounting profession.

A Brokers Opinion of Value is not USPAP compliant. However, if the purpose of the valuation is to establish a listing price for the business and the methods used to determine the Brokers Opinion of Value are reasonable, then it could be argued that this is all the business owner needs. The final price is decided by the market and the ability to locate a buyer willing to pay the price for which the business sells. Additionally, the cost of a Brokers Opinion of Value is not burdensome and may save you the expense of a Standard Valuation or Full Appraisal.

Purpose of the Valuation

To be a little clearer, it is mentioned above that there are three types of valuations; the Brokers Opinion of Value, a Standard Valuation and a Full Appraisal. The type of valuation to choose would depend on the purpose of the valuation. The Brokers Opinion of Value is mainly used by a business owner to understand the listing price of the business.

A Standard Valuation or a Full Appraisal would be requested depending on the reason for the valuation. If a matter is going to court for litigation, generally a Full Appraisal would be requested so there is a thorough examination of all aspects of the business. The other purposes of a Standard Valuation or Full Appraisal could be:
- ✓ Establishing the value of a minority owners portion of the business
- ✓ Agreeing on a value to settle a divorce
- ✓ Starting or maintaining an employee stock ownership program
- ✓ Settling a Buy/Sell Agreement
- ✓ Establish the initial value of the business to start a Buy/Sell Agreement

Valuations are also required by finance companies before they will approve a loan. But the finance companies would order the valuation and define the terms of the valuation. Hence, as I already mentioned, the result of the valuation could be different even if it is done by the same appraiser on the same business, because it depends on the purpose of the valuation.

Valuation Methods

Valuations are based on either the Market method, the Cost or Income method or the Asset method—or a combination of any or all of these. Within each method there are different valuation approaches as determined by the appraiser. This may be argued, but for privately held business valuations, the International Business Brokers' Association arrives at the value of a business called the Most Probable Selling Price or MPSP.

The MPSP comes from the Fair Market Value of tangible assets plus intangible assets plus goodwill, then plus or minus any other adjustments. Fair Market Value (FMV) is a common standard used by professional appraisers when valuing a business. Business brokers affiliated with the International Business Brokers Association generally use MPSP as the standard. The main difference between MPSP and FMV is that MPSP considers either the buyer or seller or both to be under a compulsion to make a decision, and so this affects the final price they are willing to pay or accept. FMV is the amount that the business would change hands between a willing seller and a willing buyer, when neither is under compulsion, and when both parties have reasonable knowledge of the facts of the business.

Discretionary Earnings

When conducting an appraisal for a business, the basis of the valuation generally comes from determining the Discretionary Earnings the business generates, generally over the last three years of the business operating. Discretionary Earnings has different names including Discretionary Cash Flow (DCF) and Owners Discretionary Earnings.

Explaining Discretionary Earnings is a subject in its own right and too much information for this guide. However, if it is an important subject to you and you would like to understand this topic a little more, Section Nine demonstrates how Discretionary Earnings are calculated. It also includes a template for you to try and calculate Discretionary Earnings along with a sample to show you how it is done.

Phantom Assets

An interesting question which comes up a lot for business owners and getting their business valued, is what is included in the selling price. This may seem obvious, but that isn't always the case. Most sellers will say that the price includes the customer list, fixtures, furniture and equipment (FF&E), inventory, and vehicles (if applicable). Plus, most sellers believe they have something "unique" that makes their business special, and they should therefore be paid extra.

For example, the business is on a street corner, it has 20,000 cars passing it every day, the employees are the best trained and deliver the best service in the county or have been in business 45 years. The reality is that you have been paid for these unique factors as is currently reflected in your bottom line. The point is that you cannot expect to be paid for it twice and a buyer looking to buy a business will decide what "valuation propositions" are important to them, and reflect it in their offer to buy the business.

Types of Buyer

Each buyer who inquires about your business will probably have their own unique reason for wanting to buy. By talking with the buyer, understanding their needs, and then placing them in one of the categories below, you can understand what they are looking for so you are better prepared to discuss and negotiate the transaction.

Individual Buyer

This is generally one person with good financial resources and background or experience for managing and leading a particular business in a particular industry. This type of buyer is usually looking for a particular business that is financially healthy. They are looking for a return on their investment and some flexibility in lifestyle choices. They also believe they can buy and at least maintain the current performance of the business or take it to a higher level.

Corporate Executive

This is a buyer who has many years of service with a large corporation and has concerns that downsizing may occur. In some cases, they are getting older and have their retirement money tucked away, and would like to see what it would be like to run their own business. Franchise businesses are particularly attractive to them as they like the structure and organization that comes from working in this business model.

Existing Employee

The buyer of a business can be an existing employee. If the business has a strong cash flow and the employee is able to put together a small down payment with the seller carrying back some of the financing, this can be a mutually beneficial arrangement. SBA financing may be an option here—especially if the employee has management expertise.

Investment Buyer or Financial Buyer

All buyers want a return on their investment. However, with investment or financial buyers this is their primary motivation. Their ability to get financing on as large part of the purchase price as possible is also motivating. They have less interest in the type of industry and many of the specifics of the business operation.

Synergistic Buyer

This is usually a company and their purpose of buying the business is their belief that joining the two companies will produce more, or be worth more together, than if the two companies were to remain separate.

Industry Buyer

This type of buyer is often a competitor or owns a very similar operation. They know the industry well and therefore see little value in paying for the expertise and skill of the seller.

Strategic Buyer

Like the synergistic buyer, the strategic buyer is usually a business owner with a goal to expand their current company. They leverage their expertise to enter into new markets by acquiring market share and then increase market share through the acquisition. Their strategy can also include deploying a new technology and/or eliminating a competitor or some competitive element.

Transaction Documents

The sale of any business involves a large quantity of documents. The more complex the sale, the more documents will be required. In simple terms, the documents include those used in the normal course of running the business such as Profit and Loss Statements, Balance sheets, property lease, and business tax returns.

Below is a list of the more common documents broken into three groups.
1. Documents the seller would bring to the transaction
2. Documents the buyer would bring to the transaction
3. Documents needed to be completed during the transaction

This information will allow you to collect the documents you will need and research the ones you are not sure about.

Seller Supplied Documents:
- ✓ Profit and Loss Statements for the last three years
- ✓ Balance Sheets for the last three years
- ✓ Statements of Cash Flow (if available)
- ✓ Tax returns for the last three years
- ✓ Sellers Disclosure
- ✓ List of Fixtures, Furniture & Equipment
- ✓ Confidentiality Agreement
- ✓ Resolutions to Sell
- ✓ State Sales Tax returns (if applicable)
- ✓ State Payroll Tax records (if applicable)
- ✓ List of vendors
- ✓ Confidential Business Review

Buyer Supplied or Completed Documents:

- ✓ Signed Confidentiality Agreement
- ✓ Financial statement to show the buyer has the ability to buy the business or make the down payment they are representing
- ✓ Resume to show any skill specialties (if the seller or lender requires)
- ✓ Credit report to assure the seller that the buyer has the ability to get a loan
- ✓ Buyer's Disclosure Statement

Note: If a business requires a conditional license or permit, for example, a permit that precludes the owner from holding a license if they have a felony conviction, then it would be worth requiring the buyer to make a disclosure so time is not wasted on a transaction that can never close.

Other Documents Used During the Transaction

- ✓ Asset Purchase Agreement or Letter of Intent
- ✓ Counter Offer form
- ✓ Bulk Sale information (if applicable)
- ✓ Inventory final count and value
- ✓ Bill of Sale
- ✓ Landlord Waiver (if applicable)
- ✓ Escrow instructions
- ✓ Asset Purchase Price Allocation (if applicable)
- ✓ Fictitious Name Abandonment form (if applicable)

Sources of additional information include:

www.business.gov
www.findlaw.com
www.lawyers.com
www.copyright.gov
http://www.businesslaw.gov

SDE or SDCF

If you've started your business from scratch and have a genuine buyer interested in buying your business - congratulations! The next step is the most logical and it's getting a valuation. However, before you rush out and do that, there's a few things to understand. First, you can get a valuation or appraisal to arrive at a value but this differs to a price and what the business is worth. Am I playing with words? Not intentionally and so here's the distinction.

A business appraisal or valuation will arrive at a value. That value is a defensible number the appraiser puts together from data points provided by the owner of the business such as tax returns, profit and loss statements, balance sheets, questions and answers to a series of questions such as salaries paid to the owner, hours the owner works, what non business expenses go through the business, what non recurring expenses happened in the business over the last 3 years, etc. The valuation will arrive at a value but it doesn't mean this is the number or price a willing buyer will offer for the business and conversely, it doesn't make a price the willing seller is prepared to accept. What complicates all of this is the intangibles of both the buyer and seller. If the buyer works for a corporation that is getting ready to downsize, his motivations would be different if he had just signed a 5 year employment contract. Conversely, the seller who just signed new contracts for new business may not be willing to accept the valuation and so the point I make here is that there are many variables. Once those variables make sense the challenge is then breaking down the offer to see if parties are willing to do a deal. For example, the owner may want all cash. That should lower the price paid. The seller may want a 3 year employment contract – that may increase or decrease the price – and so it goes on.
Bottom line: working through these variables is one of the most confusing pieces and often requires the help of a professional.

An important topic that goes with this discussion is Sellers Discretionary Earnings (SDE) or Sellers Discretionary Cash Flow (SCDF), or other acronyms such as EBITDA. These are important terms to understand. A business value can come from adding up the value of the assets of the business, looking at how much income the business generates or how much similar types of businesses have sold and this is called the Market Approach, or a combination of some or all of the above.

If you were a business broker performing a valuation on a business, you would take all of the data you've just collected and do a financial analysis that includes recasting to arrive at the Discretionary Earnings of the business. Once the Discretionary Earnings have been established, further research is done to determine the Most Probable Selling Price of the business.

Your goal at this point is to make sure your buyer is motivated and get an agreement on what assets in the business are being sold and who to contact to get a valuation. There will be a cost to get these valuations and different appraisers are required for different valuations. For example, if the business includes real estate you will need a commercial property appraiser. If it's just the business being sold you will need a business appraiser. If you have a large number of assets in the business such as machinery and/or office furniture you would need to get a Machinery and Equipment Appraisal. If your business has a lot of trademarks, copyrights, service marks or patents you may need the services of an appraiser that values Intellectual Property or IP.

If you decide to get a valuation make sure it is USPAP compliant. USPAP stands for Uniform Standards of Professional Appraisal Practice. USPAP rules and regulations come from The Appraisal Foundation which came into existence from an Act of Congress. The Appraisal Foundation develops, publishes, interprets and amends the USPAP standards so when appraisals are done by different appraisers, for consistency, they follow the standards set by USPAP to arrive at their value.

Your goal at this point in the transaction, as the seller of your business and its assets, is to make sure you have identified what is being sold and who to contact to get a valuation. Use the chart below to provide an overview of the contacts you've made and any agreed deadlines.

Task	Company to Contact	Phone Number	Contact Name	Price	Job Completion Time
Business Valuation					
Real Property Valuation					
Machinery & Equipment Valuation					
Intellectual Property Valuation					

Due Diligence

Once the buyer and seller have negotiated and agreed on terms for the selling of the business, in writing, the buyer would now be able to conduct due diligence to prove to their satisfaction that all claims made by the seller about the business are true and correct. This includes looking at all financial statements anywhere from the last 3 to 5 years, legally binding documents such as a lease, employment contracts etc. A good agreement should detail what the buyer wants to see as well as what the seller wants. It should also require the buyer to provide proof that he/she has a cash down payment to open escrow plus a copy of the buyer's credit score if obtaining a loan, or the seller is providing any financing.

A comprehensive checklist is provided over the next three pages. The list is extensive so not all items will apply to your situation. You may need to add your own items as they relate to your transaction, but the checklist should give you a great start. Also, be sure to make a list of any items you would like the buyer to disclose to you.

Write down questions you have about the due diligence process.

Due Diligence Checklist

Organizational Matters

1. Articles of Incorporation amendments/ restatements.

2. Bylaws/amendments.

3. Current domestic stock statement or equivalent.

4. Stock transfers ledger.

5. Buy-Sell agreements/shareholder agreements.

6. Stock restriction agreements.

7. Voting Trusts.

8. Oral understandings regarding any of the above.

Title/Lease Asset Documents

9. Real property deeds.

10. List/description of real properties owned.

11. Real property leases.

12. List/description of real properties occupied.

13. List/description of general assets (by type).

14. Bills of Sale/or invoices for equipment and/or inventory stock in trade.

15. Automobile and truck registrations.

16. List/description of automobiles and trucks owned.

17. Automobile and truck leases.

18. List/description of automobile and trucks leased.

19. Other vehicle/vessels/rolling equipment or machinery leases.

20. List/description of other vehicle/vessels/rolling equipment or machinery.

21. Office equipment leases (telephone, copy machines, etc.)

22. List/description of office equipment leased.

23. Industrial equipment leases.

24. List/description of industrial equipment leased.

25. Furniture leases.

26. List/description of furniture.

27. Patent/trademark/service mark registrations.

28. List/description of patents, trademarks and service marks.

29. Bill of Landing for inventory stock in trade.

30. List/description of inventory/stock in trade (type, item and location).

31. List/description of raw materials on hand.

32. List/description of raw materials on order.

33. Other leases or use agreements not mentioned above.

34. List/description of all other assets not mentioned above.

Encumbrances

35. Trust deeds.

36. Security agreements.

37. UCC-1 finance statements.

38. Stock pledge agreements.

39. Loan documents (including applications).

40. Notes made or held by the company.

41. Line of credit agreements.

42. Guarantees (company and personal).

43. Notices of default.

44. Oral understandings regarding any of the foregoing.

Licenses/Permits

45. City business licenses/permits.

46. City industrial/occupational permits.

47. State industrial/occupational permits.

48. State licenses/permits.

49. Federal licenses/permits (FCC, etc).

50. Correspondences to/from any state or federal body governing the business or operations of the company.

Business Contracts

51. License agreements.

52. Royalty agreements.

53. Patent/trademark/service mark assignments.

54. Dealership agreements.

55. Distributorship agreements.

56. Vendor agreements.

57. Supplier agreements.

58. Consulting agreements.

59. Employment agreements.

60. Independent contractor agreements.

61. Asset sale/purchase agreements.

62. Employee stock sale/purchase agreements.

63. Employee stock subscription agreements.

64. Employee stock option plans.

65. Employee stock option agreements.

66. Pension/profit sharing trust or agreements.

67. Medical/reimbursement plans, agreements.

68. Trust indentures.

69. Oral understandings regarding any of the foregoing.

Litigation/Adverse Claims

70. Plaintiff suits – pleadings, discovery, etc.

71. Defendant suits – pleadings, discovery, etc.

72. Attorney audit response letters.

73. Demand letters received/sent.

74. Labor board proceeding documents.

75. Administrative court proceeding documents.

76. Notices of default received.

77. Foreclosure/private sale documents.

78. Collection letters/dunning letters utilized (form or otherwise).

79. Collection letters/dunning letters received.

80. Bankruptcy filing documents.

Financial/Tax

81. Three (3) years prior state tax returns.

82. Three (3) years prior Federal tax returns.

83. Franchise tax board suspension review documents.

84. Real property tax assessment notices/documents.

85. Personal property/business equipment tax assessment notices/documents.

86. Three (3) years prior financial statements.

87. Interim financial statements.

88. Tax delinquency notices.

89. Audit inquiry response letters.

90. Summary of all deposit accounts, savings accounts and other accounts.

91. Six (6) month prior bank statements (all accounts).

92. Daily check registers/account books (including computer stored information).

93. General ledger books (including computer stored information).

94. Special account ledge books.

95. Chart of accounts.

96. Daily/weekly chronological financial records.

97. Copy of credit reference materials provided by vendors, etc.

98. List of company credit cards and holders.

99. List of vendors supplying company on account (with balances and A/R aging).

100. Ledgers showing company A/R with aging.

101. Ledgers showing company A/P with aging.

Securities

102. State securities permits/notices/filings.

103. State securities registrations/ qualifications.

104. Federal securities registration/offering circulars/disclosure documents.

105. Federal securities compliance documents (10K, 10Q, etc.)

106. Correspondence to/from the New York department of corporations.

107. Correspondence to/from the SEC.

108. Correspondence to/from any foreign body governing securities matters.

General

109. Attorney retainer letters/ correspondence.

110. Attorney opinion letter prepared with regard to the company.

111. Accountant retainer letter/ correspondence.

112. Accountant "working papers" pertaining to previous three (3) years financial statements.

113. Insurance policies including business liabilities, disability, medical and workers compensation policies.

114. Detail of key management employees: names, addresses, ages, work experience, positions held, job description, salary and benefits.

115. General information regarding employees: number of employees (full-time and part-time) by each location and department, percentage of employees who have left company and reasons for departure, working hours and wage levels by position and department.

116. Past history of labor problems.

117. Details of employees benefits (pensions, bonuses, retirement plans, etc.)

118. Policy manuals or materials.

119. Company operational or procedure manuals or materials.

120. Employee manuals or materials.

121. Employment applications and hiring forms, documents or materials.

122. Employment disclosure documents.

123. Past and present business plans for company.

124. Full organizational chart of company.

125. Details of internal operational structures including identity of who plans, checks and carries out functions, who reviews their results, and how the foregoing is accomplished:

a. Management structure,

b. Marketing structure,

c. Purchasing structure,

d. Merchandising structure,

126. Particular details of marketing/sales structures, methods and programs, including identity and functions of sales personnel, special or unusual promotional activities, occasional programs and other special sales efforts.

127. Materials or substantial contracts of agreements (written or oral) not listed above or otherwise disclosed.

What's Great About My Business!

Your business is unique. This is especially true to you as you have worked it, loved it, and lived it. So, what gets you out of bed every morning to tackle your day and go to work in your business, and to make a difference? Make a note in the table below of the items that are important to you so you can mention these to a potential buyer as an ice breaker. These items will be of interest to buyers as part of their decision-making process.

If you cannot think of at least three reasons you love your business, then I'd consider closing down the business rather than selling it. ☺

	Highlights	Why
1		
2		
3		
4		
5		
6		
7		
8		
9		
10		

Review Your Options

There's only a need to move to this section "Review your options" if your business plan is up to date and you have a buyer showing an interest in acquiring your business. If this is the case then basically you have three options. These include:

1. Stay the course and keep going. For whatever reason, you feel as though continuing to run the business and remaining the owner is the best option available to you.
2. Negotiate the best offer you can from the buyer in front of you.
3. Perhaps you hadn't considered this one, and I am definitely suggesting that you should, put the business into the market to see if you are getting the best price possible for the business.

Before you make a final decision, I would recommend that you do some brainstorming to uncover all your options. Do your own meaningful due diligence on your situation so you fully understand the options. Bring all your research together and then discuss it in depth with your immediate family so you can make a final decision and move forward … whatever that looks like to you. Make sure you review all outstanding questions (and there should be) so you get them on the table and resolved.

As part of your research, I also recommend you use the next two ideas. They are designed to provide you with a snapshot of where you are, highlight any areas you'd like to work on to research further, and so be fully prepared for making your final decision.

The first piece is a quick and dirty SWOT analysis. A SWOT analysis looks at Strengths, Weaknesses, Opportunities, and Threats.

The second piece is something I call a Reality Check. Its purpose is to allow you some time to pause, look at all the data you've collected and analyzed so far, and make that final decision.

SWOT Analysis

A SWOT Analysis helps you identify strengths, weaknesses, opportunities or threats to selling the business. This allows you to decide whether or not to move forward with the listing of the business for sale or where you are in the process in case there are issues to resolve.

Strengths will increase the selling price while weaknesses and threats will reduce the price. Opportunities can go either way. As the seller you can elect to take the opportunities and execute them to add value to the business and therefore increase the price you will get for the business. Alternatively, you can share them with a buyer so the buyer takes advantage of them as one of their motivating factors to buy your business.

Use some of the prompts below and place them in one of the boxes— strength, weakness, opportunity or threat. Make sure you add your own depending on what you think is important in relation to the industry and the business you are in.

Once you've completed the exercise, consider looking at the items in the threat box and decide if you want to work on them before trying to sell the business. Again, make sure you brainstorm other "deal points" and place them in one of the boxes so you can do a final review and take any further action you deem necessary.

Considerations for Your SWOT Analysis

- ✓ State of the national, but more importantly, the local economy
- ✓ Industry - growing or contracting?
- ✓ Business - growing or contracting?
- ✓ Interest rates - declining or increasing?
- ✓ Is yours an interest rate-sensitive business?
- ✓ Lease – can you get one in line with market and with renewal options?
- ✓ Business style - hands on with the management of the business and is this what you want?
- ✓ Is there trained management in place if the owner leaves?
- ✓ Employees - regular training program in place?
- ✓ Employees - is turnover above or below market average?
- ✓ Operations manual - does the business have one?
- ✓ Financial statements - well maintained or needing attention?
- ✓ Customer base - increasing or decreasing?
- ✓ Taxes paid in full?
- ✓ Inventory level - above or below industry average?
- ✓ Appearance of the business – is this important to you?
- ✓ Location of business?
- ✓ Good or bad public image of the industry and is this important to you?

Strength	Weakness
Opportunity	Threat

Reality Check

Now is your opportunity to sit back and look through the previous sections to review your notes and re-read what you have done to date. The next step is then to decide your best course of action.

The table below suggests some options with additional lines for you to add other options/ideas. Put a score of 1 to 10 in the right hand column next to each option. The more you like the idea, the higher the score. After you assign all scores, discard the lower scores and focus on the higher scores to make your final decision on your next steps...and then take action.

Option	Score
Do nothing – continue operating the business as is	
Sell to the buyer who has shown an interest and made an offer	
Put the business to the market to see if it will get a higher selling price	
See if I can find a partner who will help expand the growth of the business	

Other Options

If your reality check suggests the business is not yet ready to list for sale as it is not at it is optimum or needs a lot of work before getting to a saleable position, consider some other options. These could include:

1. Bringing in a partner.
2. Selling to employees.
3. Talking with your trade association to see if they have help options available
4. There are plenty of organizations available to help you including SCORE, the Small Business Development Centers and TAB. Refer back to Section One for contact information.
5. If your reality check is that the business is upside down, that is, the business is not generating enough cash flow for you to keep the doors open, consider getting help from the Turnaround Management Association: http://www.actp.org.

Write down any thoughts you may have for further reflection and research.

Refresh Your Business Plan

The purpose of this topic at this point is purely a reminder. You've spent a considerable amount of time and energy (and a lot of money along the way) with your company so it's time to bring your business plan up to date, see what's outstanding, and make a determination of whether or not you need to re-align some of your goals and communicate those to your team. It should also be a trigger to update your sales and marketing plan and revisit your financial budgets – all good things to be doing to make sure your goals are attainable and you have the focus to achieve those goals.

In no particular order I would suggest that you find a quiet place, and on your own, update your business plan with as many details as you can. The ultimate goal would be to have an answer for every item on your business plan so you can see what's outstanding. In order to do that, use the following process:

1. Open your business plan.
2. Update as many areas as you can.
3. Think of any new items you need to add since you last reviewed your business plan.
4. Answer as many of these as you can.
5. Go back over your business plan to decide the importance of each of the outstanding items by assigning a 1, 2 or 3. One means it's critical and you must have an answer before you move forward. Two means it's important but it's not a roadblock. Three means it's important but it will either solve itself as you move through the process or you're not going to worry about it.
6. Now take a break.
7. Come back to your business plan and revisit just the Ones and Twos. Decide how you want to address the Ones. The One's are the current action items so leave them as One's if they are an item you must do in the current phase of this business plan.
8. Go back and revisit the Two's. All Two's must move to a One or a Three. As we said, One means it's an action for this current review of the business plan. Three means it's an action for next time.

The bottom line is that your business plan, sales and marketing plan, productivity plan, and budgets are all works in progress. As the saying goes, it takes 21 days to create a habit so keep working these documents so they become a necessary part of your business habits and ultimately its success.

With final decisions in these documents comes action – which is what everything is about. As Pablo Picasso has said: "Action is the foundational key to all success."

5 Pitfalls To Avoid When Selling Your Business

If you try to sell your business try to avoid any of the following.

1. *Presenting bad financial or incomplete financial records*

Not only will this make the buyer uncomfortable and kill any potential deal, but if they need to borrow for the transaction it will not be possible.

2. *Verifying owner perks.*

Tax minimization is real and so is proving the business cash flow. Owner's perks often make up a large portion of the business' cash flow so having the appropriate records to substantiate the perks with a strong paper trail is necessary; once again not only for the benefit of the buyer but the lender should they choose to extend finance. Poor records of owners perks will impact the final sale price so poor records equals lower selling price, good records acceptable to buyer and lender equal higher selling price.

3. *Unreported cash*

In businesses that receive a large amount of cash, unreported cash doesn't appear on the Profit and Loss or Tax Returns. Once again this will impact the final selling price of the business and may influence whether the business in fact sells. A buyer may have the perception that if the cash is not shown in the records of the business then what else isn't being disclosed.

4. *Understanding the support team and the role each plays.*

Selling or buying a business isn't generally perceived as a team sport but if things are done correctly that's exactly what it may become. One or both sides should have an accountant and an attorney as well as an intermediary such as a business broker that understands the process and how to keep everyone on track and focused. If you're considering doing all this on your own, think about what legal forms to use, who supplies what documents at what point in the process, who handles the buyers deposit and subsequent payments, who talks to the lenders, the landlords and asks the hard question of each party to keep things moving forward to conclusion, to name a very small number of the issues to address? And how do you know you are getting a good deal?

5. *Emotional rollercoaster*

Selling a business is very difficult. Buying a business is very difficult. Misunderstandings, lack of knowledge on processes, advising when it's appropriate or inappropriate to ask for certain documents, understanding what can and can't be said to employees, suppliers, creditors, lenders, and other ancillary parties are difficult on your own. Hence the value of a quality intermediary. Bottom line: recognize the emotional roller coaster of the process and use an intermediary that has the skill and knowledge you need; but above all, who you trust.

Serious Advice For Serious Sellers

If you've read this section right through to this point and you have a genuine buyer who is interested in buying your business, your head will probably be spinning and your emotions all over the map. You've started, labored, caressed, guided and you succeeded in getting your business to this point and you've now come to a fork in the road – will I sell the business and let go of the daily control or stay where I am and continue with what I am doing.

As you work through the many variables consider the following:

1. *Don't make a final decision until you have a written binding offer.*

If you've been approached to sell your business it can be very easy to get caught up in the emotion, especially if you were not seriously looking for a buyer. Under normal circumstances I would expect your buyer to be a larger company that has the capacity to move your business into their operation. If this is the case, look for two separate and distinct things. The most important thing you may be looking for is their offer price. However, I would suggest that the most important thing you should be looking for is the terms of the deal. How much cash is up front? Are they offering guaranteed employment for you to remain? If so, how much are they offering to pay and for how long? Are they requiring an earn out which means they will agree to pay you a certain amount as long as the sales or profit reaches certain threshold. Do they want you to carry a note to be paid for some of the purchase price? Is so, how much, for how long, and what sort of interest rate will they pay? Are they offering you shares in their current company so when you fold your business into theirs and it improves their bottom line, will you be able to share in that success?

2. *What's the deadline to make a final decision?*

Whether we like it or not, our human nature, our education system that taught us to hand in assignments on time, or study for an exam on a certain date, and the reinforcing of this in our business experience of attending meetings on certain days and time, and getting work done by a firm date, teaches us to prioritize our daily tasks so we get things done. Selling or buying a business is a major event. Selling a business where the seller wants as much as possible and the buyer want to pay as little as possible can be difficult if there is no deadline to make a final decision. As you work through your transaction and to avoid the constant distraction of thinking about selling your business, if the opportunity comes along, put deadlines in place so it's clear to all parties in the transaction if a deal is or isn't being done.

3. *Don't settle until it ALL makes sense…or move on.*

While you are the only one who is being approached to sell, if at any stage in the transaction things aren't making sense, clarify them quickly or move on. A distracted owner who has to deal with employees, suppliers, customers, lenders and others in making medium to long term decisions, does not want to be distracted too long or opportunities will be lost. A key employee may find out the business is for sale and decide they are better off looking for another job in case the company that acquires them doesn't need that skill set or already has it with the other company.

Also, slowing down or delaying a response can be a negotiating tactic. If the buyer knows absolutely everything about the business that is important to them and they aren't concerned whether or not they buy the business, this can affect how quickly and thoroughly they reply to your follow up. Be careful how you handle this one. If you appear over-anxious they may try to offer a lower price. If you appear uninterested or ambivalent, they may perceive this as indifference.

Finally, if the transaction process drags out too long and some outside event happens that disrupt the economy, for example, a local earthquake or political event, this may create a distraction that leads to second thoughts in one of the parties that then scuttles the deal. So time is of the essence if you really want to sell.

4. *You will get nervous*

Selling a business is a serious decision. No one makes a serious decision without getting a little nervous. Having bought and sold five businesses and looked at many more, the nervousness helps tell me where I am at. If I don't get nervous it may mean this is not the best option for me and my family.

Can you make a good decision even if you do get nervous? You have done it many times in your life already. Good, solid, serious research and good advisers will lead you to a good decision. Do not overlook this part of the process. It's perfectly human and perfectly normal. If you are still unsure, ask immediate family and friends for their thoughts but keep your audience small. Everyone you speak with will have an opinion so four 4 opinions is twice as much work as two.

Random Q & A

Q: What is your best piece of practical advice to someone starting their business?

A: Spend time up front doing the research. Once the business opens you move into "doing" mode which takes you away from the planning mode. Also, make sure the business fits your lifestyle—and that it is something you will enjoy doing—and it will make the money your business plan projects.

End Of Chapter Notes

Use this page to write down notes, ideas and other brainstorming for starting your business.

Additional Resources &Tools

"Action is the foundational key to all success."

Pablo Picasso

Introduction

The following introduces a few different options that may be of interest to a seller when looking for sources of third party finance. The information could also be given to a buyer so they can explore further themselves. Third party finance options are many and varied but here a few highlights.

It is also not unusual for a small business transaction to incorporate a mix of funds. For example, the buyer puts down 15% of the purchase price, the seller carries back 10% and the balance of the purchase price comes from a third party loan from a lender. Like all things in the deal, this is a negotiation.

SBA Program And Other Finance Options

SBA Program

The Small Business Administration (SBA) has a range of loan programs available for qualifying businesses. There are two types of lenders: a Non-Preferred Lender and a Preferred Lender. Finding a Preferred Lender is generally the best option as these lenders are empowered to make credit decisions for the SBA. Preferred Lenders include banks, national lenders such as CIT, and popular small business and regional lenders such as Comerica and PNC.

There are extensive rules and regulations to follow that cover the SBA loan program and the lenders are also subject to conflicts of interest and ethical requirements. For example, it is very difficult for a buyer to borrow funds if they have a federal felony conviction. It is also highly unlikely to obtain a loan approval if it is to buy "a house of ill-repute," as it was called in the old days. Sex may sell but it doesn't mean you can get an SBA loan to borrow money to buy a business that engages in it.

To purchase a small business, the loan is usually either a 7(a) or 504 loan. A 7(a) loan is available to purchase a business between $25,000 and $2,000,000. However, a lot of lenders are not interested in loans under $100,000 due to the high cost of processing and meeting compliance requirements. If real estate is involved, a 504 loan would be used and the deal can go up to $6,000,000 in total finance.

For a buyer to be eligible for an SBA loan they must:
- ✓ Intend to run the business (it must be owner operated, not an investment),
- ✓ Be a US citizen (resident aliens may apply but INS gets involved, taking more time),
- ✓ Be at least 21 years old
- ✓ The business must have cash flow to meet the debt service.

For more information on the SBA programs, visit: http://www.sba.gov or send me an email to info@andrew-rogerson.com so I can connect you with a lender.

Other finance options

BORSA

BORSA stands for Business Owners Retirement Savings Account. This is a tool which allows you to fund the business start up, purchase a franchise or buy business property using your holdings in your 401(a) pension, profit sharing 401(k), 403(b), 457, IRA rollover or Roth IRA. Through the utilization of a BORSA, these purchases can be accomplished without distributions, taxes, penalties or the use of loans.

A leading provider of BORSA programs is DRDA. You can get more information from their website at http://www.drdacpa.com.

Guidant Financial Group

Another source of funds for your business startup that is similar to option one above that is to use the existing funds in your IRA. Guidant Financial Group is able to advise you on how to use a self-directed structure to access your retirement funds.

For more information, visit the Guidant website at http://www.guidantfinancial.com.

SD Cooper

Your 401K or IRA account may be used to fund the startup of a new business. SD Cooper provides a service that allows you to put the right structure in place. For more information, visit their website at http://www.sdcooper.com.

"Apply yourself. Get all the education you can get, but then, by God, do something. Don't just stand there, make it happen."

Lee Iacocca

Associations Of Interest

Trade associations can be a wonderful source of help and information for a business owner just starting out. Not only can you get direct and meaningful industry and market help from the people who work at the association, but also from the members who are business owners like you. And like you they started their business life in your industry not knowing much, so if you find a similar minded person to you (or a number of them) you have access to some wonderful and immediate knowledge.

A lot of associations publish a newsletter that offers industry resources and informative articles. Some may also offer additional benefits such as networking opportunities, discounts on goods and services, and even business and health insurance.

Find out if your industry has its own trade organization. In many cases, there may be several organizations to choose from. For example, I have the International Business Brokers Association at a national and international level but I also have a California Business Brokers Association.

If you aren't aware of associations in your field, start asking around. Make sure you evaluate the services provided by each organization and determine if the membership fee is worth the return on investment. Remember too that membership dues qualify as a business expense on your tax return.

If you've asked around and can't find an association, sit down with your computer and start doing a search. Just use key words as they relate to your industry followed by the word "association." You may be surprised at what you find. Once that is complete, do the same keyword search but replace the word association with conference. You may find some wonderful events to attend that can give you a huge and quick insight into your industry.

A couple of other reminders. Don't forget about your local Chamber of Commerce. This is an excellent place to receive support for your business and to network with business owners in your community.

There is also SCORE and Small Business Development Centers. Don't be afraid to give them a call or send them an email.

Evaluate Trade Associations

Use the template below to gather some information about associations or groups you think would be beneficial to you. There is a cost to join plus attending their events does require your time, so you need to be sure you are getting a good return on your investment.

List some associations for your industry and compare the benefits:

Association Name:	
Annual Fee:	
Number of Members:	
Regional Meetings?	
Annual Conference?	
Newsletter – Monthly or Quarterly?	
Benefits:	

Association Name:	
Annual Fee:	
Number of Members:	
Regional Meetings?	
Annual Conference?	
Newsletter – Monthly or Quarterly?	
Benefits:	

Association Name:	
Annual Fee:	
Number of Members:	
Regional Meetings?	
Annual Conference?	
Newsletter – Monthly or Quarterly?	
Benefits:	

Additional Sources Of Information

Attorney

American Bar Association	http://www.abanet.org/forums/franchising
Find a lawyer	http://www.lawyers.com
General law questions	http://www.findlaw.com

Books

Small Business Books	http://www.smallbizbooks.com
Amazon	http://www.amazon.com
Borders	http://www.borders.com
Books Online	http://www.booksonline.com

Coaching/Knowledge

Business.com	http://www.business.com
Franklin Covey	https://www.franklincoveycoaching.com
The Alternative Board	http://www.tabboards.com
Society of Competitive Intelligence Professionals	http://www.scip.org

Franchise Association

International Franchise Association:	http://www.franchise.org
Information on publicly traded franchises	http://www.edgar.gov

General Business Websites

Small Business Administration	http://sba.gov
IRS	http://www.irs.gov
Yahoo Finance	http://finance.yahoo.com
MSN Money	http://moneycentral.msn.com/home.asp
Stat-USA	http://www.stat-usa.gov
The Deal	http://www.thedeal.com
The Wall Street Journal	http://online.wsj.com/small-business
National Dialogue on Entrepreneurship	http://www.publicforuminstitute.org/nde

Leadership

Center for Entrepreneurial Leadership Clearinghouse on Entrepreneurial Education	www.celcee.edu
CEO Express	http://www.ceoexpress.com/default.asp

Magazines

Inc. Magazine	http://www.inc.com
Success Magazine	http://www.success
Entrepreneur Magazine	http://www.entrepreneur.com
Forbes Magazine	http://www.forbes.com
Business Week	http://www.businessweek.com

Other Resources

Small Business Development Center (SBDC)
The Small Business Development Centers provide management assistance to small businesses. To find your local SBDC office, check here: http://sbdcnet.org/sbdc.php

SCORE - Service Corp Of Retired Executives (SCORE)
This national organization has local chapters full of experienced business professionals that have "been there, done that" and wish to give back to their local business community by providing a free consultation/mentoring service.
For more information about SCORE: http://www.score.org
To find a local chapter near you: http://www.score.org/explore_score.html

Chambers of Commerce
http://www.uschamber.com

The Learning Annex
http://www.learningannex.com

Business Publications

Business magazines provide interesting articles and resources for business owners. There is much you can learn from reading these inexpensive publications. Visit your local bookstore or library to see samples of the various magazines available and then subscribe to one or two of your favorites. Here are some publications to consider:

Entrepreneur Magazine:	www.entrepreneur.som
Home Business Magazine:	www.homebusinessmag.com
Small Business Opportunities:	www.sbomag.com
Fortune Small Business (FSB):	www.fortune.com/fortune/smallbusiness
Inc. Magazine:	www.inc.com

"Working hard overcomes a whole lot of other obstacles. You can have unbelievable intelligence, you can have connections, you can have opportunities fall out of the sky. But in the end, hard work is the true, enduring characteristic of successful people."

Rear Admiral Marsha Evans

End Of Chapter Notes

Use this page to write down notes, ideas and other brainstorming for starting your business.

Glossary

The following glossary references some of the terms you may come across in your journey of starting your own business and then selling it.

- **Account:** In the bookkeeping sense, account means a basic category of information in which the financial effects of transactions are recorded. For example, consider a checkbook. It provides an account or itemization of the cash inflows and outflows of the balance of your checking account such as health expense, rent expense, entertainment expense, cash, etc.

- **Accounting Method:** A process under which income and expenses are determined for tax purposes. This includes both the cash and accrual procedures.

- **Accounting Period:** The 12-month period that a taxpayer uses to determine federal income tax liability.

- **Accounts Payable (AP):** Amount of money owed to suppliers by the owner of the business that are not paid for by cash but on terms of credit agreed to by both parties.

- **Accounts Receivable (AR):** Amount of money owed by customers to the owner of the business that is not paid for by cash but on terms of credit agreed to by both parties.

- **Accrual Method of Accounting:** One of the two most common methods of accounting. Under this method, income is reported in the tax year earned, whether or not received, and deductions are claimed in the tax year incurred, whether or not paid.

- **Accrued Interest:** Interest that has been earned but not yet paid or credited.

- **Acknowledgement of Receipt definition:** The last page of an Offering Circular which indicates the receipt of the documents on a certain date. This when signed and returns acts as proof of the date one received the documents.

- **Advertising Fee:** Annual fee that is paid by the franchisee to the franchisor as his share of the corporate advertising expenditures. This advertising fee is charged by few franchisors only.

- **Agent:** Individual appointed who can act on behalf of the person or entity. The corporation is legally bound by the actions of the agent.

- **Amortization:** Similar to depreciation but applies to intangible assets such as leasehold improvements.

- **Approved Products:** Those products which a franchisee must but from the franchisor. It also includes products which must be bought from approved suppliers. This is done by the franchisor in order to maintain quality across all franchisees.

- **Arbitration:** A way of resolving disputes by referring it to a third party which is selected by the parties.

- **Area Development Rights:** The rights allocated to a franchisee to operate a number of franchises within a specific geographic area.

- **Area Franchise:** A franchise licensed to develop a particular area. This Area Franchisee sometimes includes performance targets and schedules. It can also include franchise sales rights.

- **Assignment Fees:** The monthly fees paid by the franchisee to the franchise company for expenses incurred by the company like corporate marketing and advertising.

- **Asset:** Anything owned that has economic value such as a truck, cash, inventory, etc.

- **Assumed Name:** *see DBA*

- **Balance Sheet (BS):** A statement of the financial status of the business on a certain date ("snapshot").

- **Basis:** The amount assigned to an asset from which gain or loss is determined for income tax purposes when the asset is sold. For assets acquired by purchase, this is cost including other allowed adjustments such as depreciation.

- **Blue Sky:** That portion of a "claimed" value or requested price that cannot be supported or generally shown to exist through the application of established valuation methodology. Blue sky is different from Goodwill.

- **Book Value:** The depreciated value of an asset found on the balance sheet. This can be calculated by subtracting accumulated depreciation from the cost of the related asset.

- **Broker:** An intermediary between the buyer and the seller. He can represent either the buyer or the seller, and in some cases even both parties.

- **Business Format Franchise:** In Business Format Franchise the franchisor gives the permission to the franchisee for use of product, service and trademark. The entire business format is also taught to the franchisee including marketing, selling, inventory, accounting and personnel procedures.

- **Capital Required:** The amount of cash one is required to have available.

- **Cash Basis Accounting:** A method of accounting wherein income and expenses are recognized, within the statements, when the business receives the income or pays the expense. *Also see Accrual Basis Accounting.*

- **Cash Flow:** Basically, the business' net income plus non-cash charges (depreciation, amortization, and depletion). It can be defined as before or after such items as taxes, debt service (interest only or principal and interest) or extraordinary items. (Should not be confused with Net Cash Flow, a.k.a. Free Cash Flow.)

- **Cash Method of Accounting:** One of the two most common methods of accounting with the other being Accrual. Under this method of accounting, income is reported in the tax year received and expenses are deducted in the tax year paid.

- **Chart of Accounts:** The formal index of all the accounts used by the business to record its transactions.

- **Conversion Franchise:** Is a franchise system permitting existing businesses to join a national franchise system to be able to use its name, trademark and operating system.

- **Copyright:** Form of protection under the law for authors to protect "original works of authorship." This protection is available for both published and unpublished works.

- **Corporation:** A legal business entity owned by shareholders with the ability to own property, incur debts and sue or be sued. For income tax purposes, this term includes associations, trusts that have a majority of corporate characteristics, joint stock companies and insurance companies.

- **Cost of Goods Sold/Cost of Sales** (CGS, COGS, COS): A grouping of expenses applicable to the materials and labor incorporated directly in the goods or services delivered and sold.

- **DBA (Doing Business As):** An assumed name under which a business conducts business. For example, Billy Bob Enterprises, Inc. DBA Billy Bob's Hot Dog Grill and Bar.

- **Default:** The failure to perform as was agreed upon by the parties.

- **Depreciation:** The deduction of a reasonable allowance for the wear and tear of assets (excluding inventory) used in a trade or business or held for the production of income.

➢ **Disclosure:** Refers to revealing facts to others. In a franchise these facts may be complimentary to the franchisor, such as disclosing a prior bankruptcy or litigation.

➢ **Discretionary Earnings:** Adjusted earnings before taxes, interest income or expense, non-operating and non-recurring expenses, depreciation and other non-cash charges and prior to deducting an owners/officers compensation.

➢ **Distributorship:** The right granted by a manufacturer or a wholesaler for distribution or sale of products. Distributorship does not generally qualify as a franchisee. However certain franchisees can qualify as a distributorship.

➢ **Domestic Corporation:** A corporation in the state where it has been incorporated.

➢ **Earnings Claims:** Assertions made by franchise companies of specific acquired sales levels or profitability levels.

➢ **EIN (Employer Identification Number):** *See Federal Tax Identification Number.*

➢ **Employee:** An individual that provides services to a business and is distinguished differently from an independent contractor. This is important because the withholding of incomes taxes on wage applies only to this individual.

➢ **Entrepreneur:** The Person who assumes the responsibility for organizing and operating the business. He also assumes the risk including the financial risk for a business venture.

➢ **Equity:** The recorded "value" of the ownership interest in a business entity. Also known as Owner's Equity.

➢ **Estimated (Useful) Life:** Period of time over which an asset will be used by a particular taxpayer.

➢ **Exclusive Territory:** Gives the right of the territory to the franchisee preventing the franchisor from appointing any other franchisee for the territory or carrying on business himself in the territory.

➢ **Expense:** An item charged against revenue in the income statement for something that is used up during the income statement period of time.

➢ **Fair Market Value (FMV):** The amount at which property would change hands between a willing buyer and a willing seller, neither being under compulsion to buy or sell and both having reasonable knowledge of the relevant facts.

➢ **Federal Tax Identification Number:** This is a number assigned to a corporation or other business entity by the federal government for tax purposes. This is also known as EIN (Employer Identification Number).

➢ **FICA (Federal Insurance Contributions Act):** The law that provides for Social Security and Medicare benefits. This program is financed by payroll taxes imposed equally on the employer and the employee. A person self-employed will pay both the employer and employee portion of this tax which is known as self-employment tax.

➢ **Fiscal Year:** Any period of exactly or approximately 12 months used by a business as its accounting period. Some retail businesses always close their yearend on a Saturday and therefore will have either 52 or 53 weeks in a fiscal year.

➢ **Foreign Corporation:** A corporation not organized under the laws of one of the states or territories of the United States. This description relates to the federal level as this term is also used by each state to describe a corporation doing business in the state but organized under another states laws.

- ➤ **Franchise:** Permission given by a person or entity permitting the distribution of goods or services under his trademark, service make to trade name by an agreement to another person or entity. During this period the grantor retains control over the franchisee.

- ➤ **Franchise Business Plan:** A strategic plan that lays down the company's objectives and the specific steps that need to be taken to achieve those objectives. The Business Plan is usually prepared by company management.

- ➤ **Franchise Fee:** Fee paid by the franchisee to the franchisor initially to acquire the franchise.

- ➤ **Goodwill:** The ability of a business to generate income in excess of a normal rate on assets due to superior managerial skills, market position, new product technology, etc.

- ➤ **Gross Profit:** That portion of Net Sales that remains after the subtraction of the Cost of Goods Sold. This is sometimes called Gross Margin.

- ➤ **Housemark:** A trademark which is used to identify the operations of an organization. This may in certain cases also be the company name. This trademark is used to identify one or more products and at times is used in combination with other trademarks.

- ➤ **Income:** All sources of business income; may be synonymous with Revenue or Sales.

- ➤ **Income Statement (IS):** A financial statement used to report the financial results of a business' operations during the period of time specified within the statement. Also known as the Profit and Loss or P&L.

- ➤ **Independent Contractor:** Taxpayer who contracts to do work according to his own methods and who is not subject to control except as to the results of such work. An employee, by contrast, is subject to the control of the employer as to the methods to be used to obtain the desired results.

- ➤ **Industry:** The category of business that a franchise belongs to. It is an all-encompassing area of business that can incorporate several different sectors.

- ➤ **Intangible Personal Property:** Assets, other than real property, with no intrinsic value; its value lies in the rights conveyed. Examples include cash, insurance, stock, goodwill, and patents.

- ➤ **International Franchise Association IFA:** Based in Washington, D.C., a trade association for franchisors.

- ➤ **Inventory:** List of articles of property. For income tax purposes, this refers only to a list of articles comprising stock in trade–articles held for sale to customers in the regular course of a trade or business.

- ➤ **Lessee:** One who rents property from another. In the case of real estate, the lessee is also known as the tenant.

- ➤ **Lessor:** One who rents property to another. In the case of real estate, the lessor is also known as the landlord.

- ➤ **Limited Liability Company (LLC):** Operating structure contains the liability protection of a corporation and the flexibility of a partnership.

- ➤ **Liquidation:** The process of converting securities or other property into cash.

- ➤ **Marketing Plan:** Detailed plan setting the marketing activities of the organization.

- ➤ **Master Franchise:** Individual or a company which owns the exclusive rights to develop a particular continent.

- ➤ **NAICS (North American Industry Classification System) Code:** A system of numbering that assigns a unique number to each business industry and thereby allows for collection and comparison of statistical information within an industry. *Also see SIC code.*

➢ **Operations Manual:** Covers all the aspects of the business and consists of guidelines for the franchisee on how to operate the franchised business.

➢ **Ownership:** A generic term meaning 100% controlling ownership.

➢ **Partnership:** Form of business in which two or more persons join their money and skills in conducting the business. This form is treated as a conduit and is not subject to taxation.

➢ **Patent:** Legal protection for an inventor. If issued, a patent grants "the right to exclude others from making, using, offering for sale, or selling" the invention. There are three types of patents: design, utility and plant.

➢ **Perquisites (Perks):** Special additional benefits received as compensation because of position. In privately held businesses these are often a result of the ability of the business to pay for them, more than a result of market rate compensation for the services provided to the business. For example, company-paid vehicles, insurance, travel, memberships, etc.

➢ **Prepaid Expense:** The capitalized payment for items such as rent, insurance, etc. that cover more than one year. Cash-basis as well as accrual-basis taxpayers usually are required to capitalize these types of costs.

➢ **Product Format Franchise:** Where the franchised product or service does not constitute the majority of the products or services on offer by the franchisee.

➢ **Pro forma statements:** Statements issued by the franchisor to the franchisee based on actual operating results of the franchisor's units or franchise establishments. It can be in the form of any statement which measures profits and expenses.

➢ **Protected Territory:** Territory allotted to a franchisee where the franchisor has promised not to franchise to another franchisee or open a company owned business.

➢ **Public Figure Involvement:** When a public figure is endorsing a franchised product then the nature of the agreement between the public figure and the franchisor must be disclosed.

➢ **Qualification Questionnaire:** a document prepared by the franchisor to seek information from a prospective franchise.

➢ **Quality Control:** The method used by the franchisor to enforce the rules set in the operating manuals. Quality control involves regional coordinators visiting each franchisee.

➢ **Royalty:** The franchisee is required to pay to the franchisor a percentage of the gross sales on a monthly basis.

➢ **S Corporation:** An elective provision permitting certain small business corporations and their shareholders to elect special income tax treatment. Of major significance is the fact that this election usually avoids the corporate income tax and corporate losses can be claimed by the shareholders.

➢ **Section 179 Expense Deduction:** An election to treat the cost of certain qualified property as a currently deductible expense rather than as a capital expenditure. This treatment is also referred to as expensing. A maximum deduction, adjusted annually, may be claimed for qualified assets placed in service during the year. This deduction may be further limited based on the total cost of depreciable assets placed in service during the year.

➢ **Sector:** The categories included within a broader scope of franchise opportunities. It is also known as the Industry.

- ➢ **SIC (Standard Industrial Classification) Code or NAICS (North American Industry Classification System) Code:** System of numbering that assigns a unique number to each business industry. This allows for collection and comparison of statistical information within an industry.

- ➢ **Slick:** Pre-paid piece of advertising material which the franchisor gives to the franchisee for use in local print media.

- ➢ **Source Documents:** Virtually every business transaction needs documentation which is known as a source document or supporting documentation (back-up). Examples include check register, invoice, receipt, purchase order, etc.

- ➢ **Start Up Costs:** The investment required to be made by the franchisee at the start of the franchise.

- ➢ **Total Investment:** Initial investment, the working capital, and subsequent additions to inventory and equipment which will be necessary for the fully operational and profitable enterprise.

- ➢ **Trade Secret:** Are revealed to the franchisee by the franchise transaction.

- ➢ **Trademark:** Word, name, symbol, or device that is used in trade with goods to indicate the source of the goods and to distinguish them from the goods of others.

- ➢ **Turnkey:** The franchisor is expected to provide the platform to run the business to the franchisee, even without any input from the franchisee.

- ➢ **Working Capital:** Excess of the value of the current assets over the value of the current liabilities.

Other Books In This Series

If you've always thought you would like to own and operate your own business but were never sure where to start, this is the guide for you. This 174 page workbook starts by asking the question if business ownership is for you. It then explains the options available to you and then takes you through, in detail, a step by step process to determining what sort of business you can buy, what you will need to buy a business, and, how to evaluate a business for sale. It also includes the steps to prepare for business ownership with your legal entity, understanding business licenses and permits, how to obtain finance to buy a business, accounting processes and terms, financial planning tools such as profit and loss projectors, sales forecasts, how to create business plans, sales and marketing plans. There are lots of checklists, resources, other planning sheets and tools so when you buy your business you are up and running as quickly as possible for maximum profit.

If you are considering business ownership there are three options available to you. Start your own business from scratch, buy an existing business or buy the rights to a franchise in your local market. This 144 page guide is for those who are considering buying a franchise. The processes can be very confusing and demanding trying to work out the many variables such as which franchise to buy, what franchises are available, what is the initial cost, how much are the royalties and any other ongoing costs and which legal entity to use. It also looks at getting a loan, what the franchisor provides, your role, how much and what sort of support you get. This guide covers all these questions and many more. If you are serious about buying a franchise this guide will walk you through the steps and provide the answers for you from the initial steps to opening the doors of your business while answering all your questions so you do things from a position of strength.

Thinking about selling your business? This 150 page comprehensive workbook helps you understand the many complexities and decisions you have to make. Written by a professional business broker with many years of real world business experience, this guide shows you how to sell your business in the shortest possible time for the best possible price. It includes reasons why you need to plan ahead for taxes, how to avoid potential legal, accounting, and other roadblocks, how to value your business and other assets, the different types of professionals available and how to research and properly prepare for selling. Also includes how to search for and qualify potential buyers, address finance concerns, protect you and your business with confidentiality agreements, prepare an executive summary, confidential business review and conduct effective negotiations. Also includes dozens of worksheets, checklists, and charts for you to track during the steps of selling.

About The Author

Andrew Rogerson currently holds the Certified Business Intermediary (CBI) designation from the International Business Brokers Association (IBBA), the highest designation awarded by the IBBA. Andrew has also earned the Certified Business Broker (CBB) designation from the California Association of Business Brokers. He holds a Certified Machinery and Equipment designation (CMEA) from the National Equipment and Business & Builders Institute and is a Certified Senior Business Analyst (CSBA) with the Society of Business Analysts. Andrew also has a Brokers license with the California Department of Real Estate.

As the owner and managing director of a Sacramento office of Murphy Business and Financial Corporation, a franchise based in Clearwater, Florida, Andrew assists his clients with both selling and buying businesses.

Since 1983, Andrew has owned and operated five businesses. At just 27 years-old, he bought his first business, an international travel agency. With hard work resulting in increased sales, Andrew sold the travel agency just two years later for 2 1/2 times his original purchase price.

Andrew's next venture involved owning and managing two retail office equipment/furniture stores, followed by a wholesale travel and tourism company based in Los Angeles that had an annual turnover of $10,000,000. More recently, Andrew and his wife Anne owned an executive suites business in Fair Oaks, CA. Anne operated this business while Andrew worked as an outsourced program manager at the Roseville campus of Hewlett Packard. At HP, Andrew managed a team of 42 employees, deploying a new global call center and support team that included Web developers, technical writers and trainers.

Andrew was educated at La Trobe University in Melbourne, Australia, his native country, and recently completed studies in Business Valuation and Appraisals and Business Brokerage. Andrew and Anne have two daughters, Belinda and Catherine and reside in Sacramento, California. Andrew enjoys flying (he is pursuing his pilot's license) and SCUBA diving as well as sports and politics.

Contact Andrew for Assistance with Buying or Selling a Business

Andrew offers a broad range of services including business valuations, transaction analysis, consulting for business sellers and buyers, consulting for buyers considering franchise ownership and appraisals for machinery and equipment.

The combination of Andrew's hands-on experience in the business buying and selling process, his diverse background in a variety of industries and his international business experience makes him an ideal choice for a business intermediary.

Call Andrew Rogerson at (916) 570-2674 or send him an e-mail at info@Andrew-Rogerson.com to discuss how you can put his knowledge and experience to work for you.

Visit Andrew's website: www.Andrew-Rogerson.com